*writing*fiction

GARRY DISHER lives on the Mornington Peninsula in Victoria. A full-time writer for most of his working life, he has also taught creative writing, designed writing courses for the TAFE system and published writers' handbooks. His novels and short-story collections are widely translated and have won numerous honours, including the NSW Premier's Ethel Turner, CBC Book of the Year and German Crime Fiction awards, a Booker Prize nomination, and a listing in *Publishers Weekly*'s best books of the year in the USA. His latest novel is *Past the Headlands*.

writing fiction

AN INTRODUCTION TO THE CRAFT

GARRY DISHER

ALLEN&UNWIN

This edition extensively rewritten, revised and expanded,
published by Allen & Unwin, 2001
Second edition, revised and expanded, 1989
First published by Penguin Books Australia, 1983

Allen & Unwin
83 Alexander Street
Crows Nest NSW 2065
Australia
Phone: (61 2) 8425 0100
Fax: (61 2) 9906 2218
Email: info@allenandunwin.com
Web: www.allenandunwin.com

National Library of Australia
Cataloguing-in-Publication entry:

Disher, Garry, 1949– .
    Writing fiction: an introduction to the craft.

    [Rev. ed.].
    Bibliography.
    ISBN 1 86508 589 8.

    1. Fiction—Authorship. 2. Fiction—Technique. I. Title.

808.3

Set in 10.25/14 pt Stempel Schneidler by Bookhouse, Sydney
Printed in Australia by McPherson's Printing Group

10 9 8 7 6 5 4 3 2

for Pam Harvey
(who does not need this book)

AUTHOR'S NOTE

Writing Fiction is a substantially reworked and updated edition of my 1980s handbook of the same title. It also incorporates material from two later publications: *Writing Professionally* (Allen & Unwin, 1991) and 'Plot and Structure' in Marele Day (ed.), *How to Write Crime* (Allen & Unwin, 1996). I gratefully acknowledge the role of Jackie Yowell in commissioning this edition and helping me to rethink every sentence.

CONTENTS

CONTENTS

CONTENTS

one

BECOMING A WRITER

> *Talent is a compulsion, a critical knowledge of the*
> *ideal, a permanent dissatisfaction.*
> THOMAS MANN

This is a handbook about the craft of fiction writing for new and developing writers. It can't conjure your talent, vision and imagination, or teach you how to write, but it can encourage the awareness that may help you to be observant, develop your own voice and become a better writer.

BEFORE YOU START

A handbook on writing cannot help you unless you invest time and effort in developing your talents. For example, it's unwise to set out to be a writer of fiction without first being a *reader* of it. Yet, as writing teachers know, many beginner writers do not read much or are unfamiliar with contemporary writers and styles of fiction. Writers of fiction who are also thoughtful readers of it are better able to make informed assessments of their own work, forge their own writing styles and try a range of structural approaches.

Becoming a writer also involves patience, a readiness to rewrite, developing a resilience to rejections from publishers, and being realistic. I once spent a week writing a detailed reader's report for a man whose first novel had been rejected by a publisher. The novel had interesting characters and a moving theme, but it was too long by half, sloppily constructed and badly written. In conversation with the man I learned that the novel was the story of his life, but he had no particular perspective on his life and merely reported everything that had happened to him. The manuscript needed a major rewrite and I suggested how this might be done. I happened to mention that even if the manuscript were accepted the print run would be about 3000–5000 copies, not all would be sold, and he would earn, in a trickle of royalties, only 10 per cent of the selling price of each book sold.

He was aghast. He didn't know about the hard work, rejection slips and low income that are the lot of the professional writer but expected to make tens of thousands of dollars in hardback, paperback, film and foreign translation rights. He said, 'Forget it,' and turned to another hobby.

I believe that many new writers have false or romanticised notions about writing, the writer's life and getting published. They don't realise that writing and rewriting require thought, care, patience and long hours of solitary work; that what is easy to read has been difficult to write. As long-distance runners need training, and *ongoing* training, in order to run a marathon, writers learn to write by observing, being perceptive, reading, writing, drafting and refining, and developing good work habits.

Writers take what they do seriously. Raymond Carver, an American poet and short-story writer, once heard a fellow writer say apologetically that his latest book would have been better if he'd taken more time. Carver was appalled: '…if the writing can't be made as good as it is within us to make it, then why do it?'

If I've sounded finger-wagging in these opening remarks, I'm wagging the finger at my younger self, who was in love with the idea of being a writer but didn't write, who later dashed off stories in an afternoon and considered them finished, who wasted time on projects that tested no abilities and brought no pleasure, and who took too long to develop the habits and state of mind required to become a writer. It all seemed too hard sometimes. Now, twenty years later, writing is all I do. I think and feel like a writer, and wouldn't have it any other way. Sure, it's satisfying to make a living from something I love doing, and see my books studied, translated or optioned for films, but the main reward has been to realise that I'm getting better at what I do. I hope you find the same sense of satisfaction, and I hope this book helps.

DO YOU REALLY WANT TO WRITE?

I often hear people say, 'I don't read but I know there's a book in me', or 'I could write a book if only I had the time', or 'My life has been so interesting it would make an interesting book', or 'I don't understand all the fuss about Isabel Allende:

I could write something just as good', or 'I'm going to write a psychological mystery because they're big with publishers at the moment', or 'I was always good at English at school so I know I could write a good novel one day', or 'Now that I'm retired I think I'll write a book'.

The only possible response to these statements is, 'Do it, don't tell me about it'. It's not enough to hold a vaguely formed notion of wanting to write. As Australian poet Kevin Hart has said about the desire to write poetry, something beckons from the far side of experience. Writing comes out of a deep-seated need for self-expression and to make sense of life, tell stories, entertain, and capture what we feel when we read fiction that moves and enthrals us.

A related question is, 'Are you ready to begin writing?' Rainer Maria Rilke wrote in *Letters to a Young Poet* that he was 'almost ready' to begin writing when he was thirty, and that to write something worthwhile can take a lifetime.

I'm assuming that you badly—rather than idly—want to write, and understand that being a writer entails *becoming* a writer. Even so, I know—from my own experience, and from working with beginner writers—that there may be times when you'll need to tackle the problems of under-confidence or over-confidence.

UNDER-CONFIDENCE

You have a terrible secret, apparently one not shared by real writers: writing fills you with doubts, fears, anxieties and self-consciousness.

Perhaps the words won't come, or are not there, or your prose is stiff and mannerly, or you never finish any of your projects, or you'll do anything to avoid sitting at your desk, or you stopped writing after the first rejection slip or critical feedback, or you're waiting for wisdom to come, or you're fearful of being judged, or you think your work has to be perfect, or you never know where you're going when you start something and think real writers don't work like that, or you can't write anything unless a teacher has set the topic and deadline, or you can't be a real writer because real writers are mad, doomed, brilliant, sensitive souls who never spend their Saturdays at the laundromat.

These are the common fears of new writers, but rest assured that *all* writers experience some of them from time to time. Some of us gain equilibrium quickly, others may stop writing for long periods, a few stop forever. This is a book about the craft of writing, not soul maintenance, but I've been a writer and worked with new writers for a long time now, and know something about the fears and misconceptions of writers.

I think many new writers find themselves waiting for that flash of creative insight they believe lies behind the writing of fiction, or believe that the best writing grows out of powerful feelings and intense passion. In fact, as Chapter 3 shows, anything at all, even the most mundane incident, can give rise to a story or novel, and the best writing and creative insights often come from writing calmly and with detachment—which is not the same thing as indifference—day after day. Don't sit and wait. Start writing, and write regularly—for the practice, and to find what it is you want to say.

Also, new writers often don't trust themselves or their words—their own experiences or ways of speaking about them—and hold mistaken notions of what a short story or novel should be. Perhaps harking back to their school years they believe that 'good' writing must be 'arty', flowery or difficult to read. Others use 'literariness' and obscurity as a form of self-protection, fearing that readers might otherwise see through them. Certainly writing craft is important, but often it's the natural rather than the forced voice that sounds fresh and original. Vision, and writing assuredly, matter more than style, and will in fact impart style. New writers can often 'free' themselves by writing about a bad childhood experience in a simple, ordinary way. This might then be central to a larger work, or the key to another story. In this way we often find the story we realise is the one we wanted to tell all along.

New writers also feel anxious about planning. When Raymond Carver learned that fellow American short-story writer Flannery O'Connor usually didn't know where she was headed when she sat down to write a short story, he was 'tremendously heartened'. He'd thought only he wrote like that, and had been uneasy about it, as though it revealed his shortcomings. Paul Theroux was surprised to learn that V. S. Naipaul found writing to be 'torture', for Naipaul's work seemed so 'humorous and full of ease, the imagery precise and vivid, the characters completely human'. He later learned that to write well 'one went slowly, often backwards, and some days nothing at all happened'.

From time to time all writers find themselves knowing what to write but do anything to avoid writing. Having an idea is not the same thing as developing it on the page.

Edna O'Brien once said that the essential quality of the writing life is stasis. We dodge writing even as we seek incentives to write. We hope, mope about and make copious notes to salve our consciences. Fear is often the key to the problem: fear that we're not up to the task, fear that our writing isn't good enough, fear of making mistakes, fear of being judged. It helps to identify this fear; it also helps simply to sit down and write, for then, often, the fear will vanish and the act of writing will unlock more writing, setting further ideas free, especially if the writing is not self-conscious but a natural expression of what we feel and think.

All writers find themselves giving up from time to time. They start but never finish projects, cut from one project to another, can't relax, follow fruitless distractions. It could be that they have chosen unwieldy, difficult or boring subjects, or haven't done the necessary contemplation, planning or research, but often they are putting off the sorts of fears mentioned above.

Sometimes writers are anxious that others will see their kind of writing as narrow and limited. They write only short stories, for example, or repeat themes, settings and situations in their novels and stories. This isn't necessarily a narrowness of range. For a start, the short story should never be seen as a lesser form than the novel, and writers who know where their interests lie are luckier than writers who seek them forever or dissipate their talents trying their hand at every form or genre. Fiction writing arises from two contrary yet complementary impulses, one toward economy, efficiency and implication—the short story—and the other toward expansion and indulgence—the novel. Some writers experiment endlessly, others find style and subject early in their careers and stick to them. The fine Canadian short-story writer Alice Munro is an example of the latter. She writes only short stories, and writes mostly about small-town, small-farm life in southern Ontario.

Criticism of one's writing can be wounding, but it's important not to confuse this with a judgement of your *person*. Try to stand apart from your work and judge it calmly. Accept where you've made errors or written badly, for how else, apart from writing practice, will you learn to be a better writer? Rewriting may be difficult for new writers who are often finding their voices by writing anew each time, but it's a critical means to developing writing skills.

Try to trust your own feelings and experiences. It can be paralysing to hold the belief that you have nothing to write about because you haven't lived yet or nothing's happened in your life. As Flannery O'Connor said, 'If you've survived adolescence, you have enough to write about for the rest of your life.'

OVER-CONFIDENCE

Equally as crippling for writers is over-confidence. Over-confident writers believe that simply because they have written something it has worth, and doesn't require correction or improvement. They see writing as 'self-expression', an extension of the self, and that this makes it somehow intrinsically worthwhile. They take criticism of their writing as criticism of themselves personally. To the question, 'Can writing be taught?' they might respond, 'Can anything be learned about writing?'

While anxiety may lie at the heart of over-confidence, over-confident writers also have an insufficient sense of language as something separate from themselves, an external well from which words may be selected and artfully arranged according to techniques that can be learned and developed. They regard 'rules' as authoritarian and believe that 'creativity' comes from a divine spark, unfettered by conventions, strategies or techniques. For them there is no sense of the role that *form* plays in making *content*; no sense of language's playfulness, insinuations, shapeliness, poise, formal constraints, beauties and provocations; no sense that revision and self-editing are a natural and necessary part of the writing process.

In fact, it's through learning the 'rules'—and how to use, subvert and 'unlearn' them—that writing becomes a pleasurable, liberating act and the words effective. As the American poet Robert Frost said, when responding to someone who suggested that surely he didn't think about technical tricks as he wrote his poetry: 'Madam, I revel in 'em!' Just as writing poetry requires an understanding of factors like metre, writing fiction requires an understanding of characterisation, structure and viewpoint—even if you eventually know enough to risk dispensing with these things.

HOW THIS BOOK WORKS

The trouble with a book like this is that it has to separate out discrete elements of fiction writing, such as plot, character and setting, in order to identify them, when in fact they work interdependently during the actual writing of a short story or novel. Nevertheless, there are times, especially when we're 'blocked', rewriting or tackling a matter of technique, that we stop to ask ourselves questions like: 'Is this story heading in an unlikely direction?' or 'Is this character necessary?' or 'Have I made the house spooky enough?'

So I have taken a conventional approach to fiction writing—after all, James Joyce could only write a novel as original as *Ulysses* because he had already written the more conventional *Dubliners*. It's only through learning the basics that writers recognise how the boundaries might be extended. Nevertheless, where appropriate I do discuss some of the techniques of experimental fiction.

The advice in this book may be applied to all types of fiction writing. It challenges the notions that 'fiction writer' means 'a novelist for an adult readership', that writing short stories is merely a stepping stone to writing novels, that children's and genre (for example, romance or crime) fiction is 'lighter' or easier to write than 'serious' fiction, and that children's and genre writers are not talented enough to write 'serious' fiction. In fact, I believe that good short stories are more demanding to write than novels, and some of the most interesting fiction being published is written by children's and crime writers.

The chapters in this book are grouped loosely according to the types of material covered—for example, 'Plot' is grouped with 'Planning' and 'Structure', and 'Character' with 'Dialogue' and 'Point of View'—but no chapter can be read in isolation, for all of the aspects of fiction work together.

I often use the terms 'tension' and 'suspense'. These mean more than simply tightening the screws in a mystery or thriller novel. Almost all novels and stories rely on their effects by posing questions and maintaining doubts about outcomes.

The questions 'Will she make the same mistake?' or 'Will he get the girl?' can be made just as suspenseful for the reader as 'Who committed the murder?'

GOOD WORK HABITS

experienced writers

I write the first draft of a story or novel with a blue ballpoint pen on the backs of used A4 paper, then type it up on the computer, print it out, edit it by hand, type in the corrections and print it out again—many times. By the time a novel is ready for submission I have a wine carton full of manuscript drafts.

But does it help you to know that? We are often curious about the writing habits of published writers, as though their methods might be the key to our own artistic or financial success. Consider the following:

Saul Bellow's habit was to work every day from 7 a.m. to 1 p.m. without distractions. Colleen McCullough wrote ten drafts of *The Thorn Birds*, at times working eighteen hours a day. Anthony Trollope had a full-time job, but forced himself to write three hours a day, 10000 words a week; he wrote fifty novels in forty years. Scott Turow spent eight years writing *Presumed Innocent* while commuting to work on the morning train. Peter Carey writes up to 1500 words a day, Erica Jong 300. V. S. Naipaul always writes several drafts, including handwritten drafts of typed drafts, and threw out 20000 words of his novel, *The Mimic Men*. Michael Ondaatje writes five or six drafts by hand in notebooks before transferring the material to a computer for a further nine or ten drafts. P. D. James spends up to three years on each of her novels, half of this time on thinking and planning. Alex Miller took five years and six drafts to write *Conditions of Faith*, Sena Naslund four years and four drafts to write *Ahab's Wife*, and Roald Dahl six hundred hours over five months to write the short story, 'Mrs Bixby and the Colonel's Coat'. Gerald Murnane can spend hours on a paragraph, and he wrote seven drafts of *Landscape with Landscape*. The *Writers at Work* collections, comprising interviews that first appeared in the journal, *Paris Review*, reveal that most writers work in the mornings, but others work all day or only at night. Some write many drafts, the first quickly and subsequent ones more carefully, while others rewrite as they progress. All write regularly, every day if possible, even if they have other jobs; all know the value of rewriting; and all treat writing as hard, intermittently pleasing, work.

As these examples show, the real key is hard work, dedication and persistence. There is no trade secret. It all has to be discovered from within, through work and trial and error, and management of your twin natures—your creative side, which knows no rules, and your practical side, which criticises, edits and shapes.

practical advice

It's pointless to wait for inspiration. The brilliant idea that you jot down in your notebook at 2 a.m. or at a traffic light may be no more than a sentence that has lost its force the next time you read it, whereas sitting down every day and writing a few pages whether you feel like it or not will produce a sizeable output of work within a few months. You'll often find that writing unlocks more writing, that your mind will begin to focus and the ideas to flow once you start writing, and you can always go back and rewrite your false starts.

Try to establish a modest schedule that fits in with the other aspects of your life: for example, getting up two hours earlier or staying up two hours later; deciding upon a target of three pages or 1000 words a day; setting a deadline of twelve months to complete the first draft of your novel. Regularity is the key: it's better to write 100 words every day than have a blitz of writing once a month.

Write whether you feel like it or not. You might find that you're dependent upon a little behavioural obsession before you can start: some writers line up their pens and pads neatly, others sharpen their pencils, write standing up at a podium, play music, do exercises, drink tea, read their e-mails. Try going over the previous day's writing: this will help you to correct mistakes and absorb yourself in the voice of the work. Don't exhaust all of your material in one burst but stop at a point that allows you to go on the next day. Consider dealing with the task a day at a time. If you're writing a long work, such as a novel, don't tell yourself 'Today I'm writing my novel' but 'Today I'm starting the love scene', or 'Today I'm introducing the main character's mother'. You might write best when you're detached from the material, but you should never be indifferent to it, for this will show in the writing.

If you're 'blocked', you might find that it's better to do something related to your project than go shopping: a long walk to clear your head, for example, a trip to the library to follow up research issues, or a session of editing your manuscript. If that doesn't help, you may have to put the manuscript aside for some days or weeks and start a new project.

Try not to worry about 'talent' or the lack of it. Writing ability comes from desire, temperament and the careful management of your instincts and feelings, and can be developed over time. Paradoxically, as you become a better writer you'll become more absorbed with writing as a craft, and probably find that writing gets harder rather than easier. Michael Ondaatje has said: 'There's this illusion that if you've written four books you can write a fifth. But I always have a complete uncertainty that I can write another book, and an enormous sense of gratitude when I find I can.'

Revise, and revise again. Try to be honest. Who are you? What do you believe? Are you writing from within yourself or merely copying? Read your work aloud, perhaps onto a tape, listening for words, phrases and sentences that seem awkward or too long, and passages of dialogue that don't ring true. Correct the spelling and grammar if you can; never assume that that's the editor's job.

Not everything you write need or should be submitted to a publisher, of course. At the same time, understand that over-revision might destroy the freshness and spontaneity of your voice. The cut-off point between enough and too much revision is problematic. How does one assess that? Putting your manuscript aside and reading it with fresh eyes later is usually helpful (see Chapter 14), as is regular or systematic feedback on each manuscript draft (see below).

daily maintenance

Meanwhile, try to prepare for writing even when you are not actually doing it. Learn to be observant, sceptical, inquiring and speculative. Keep a notebook for ideas, snatches of dialogue, character sketches, descriptions and observations, and folders for useful newspaper clippings. Some of these you might never use, others you'll alter drastically; many will be vague stirrings that might be precursors of a more developed work, a few you'll sit on until another idea or image 'awakens' them.

It can take some writers years to develop a comfortable or authentic style, while in others it's there from the start. Learn to appreciate words, their sounds, meanings, playful possibilities, rhythms and conjunctions with other words. Read widely in all forms of writing, including 'junk' writing, in order to see how writers use and misuse language. Try copying out passages of writing you admire: look at them on the page and read them aloud, noting how the sentences are paced and punctuated and asking yourself why they're arranged like that and what effect it has compared to a different arrangement. Vladimir Nabokov once said: 'After many false tries, false moves, you have the sentence you recognise as the one you are looking for.'

GOING PUBLIC

getting feedback

Most writers, beginner and experienced alike, seek informed responses to their manuscripts and advice about writing craft from time to time. This is not always easy to get. A lucky few of us may develop a long-term, mutually advantageous relationship with a writer friend but, for most of us, good feedback is rare, sporadic or comes from a formal source.

In the first instance, try putting your work aside for some time (several days or weeks). When you come back to it you are bound to see it much more objectively. In this way you learn to give *yourself* feedback.

When approaching another person for feedback, try to choose someone who has experience or whose judgement you trust, bearing in mind that a loved one or friend might automatically praise your work or be reluctant to criticise it. You might also find, as I do, that when you talk to others about a book you're writing (or have to describe it in a grant application), the magic leaks away and you no longer want to write it.

It can be helpful to belong to a local writing group (a writers' organisation or local library may have details). These provide a supportive atmosphere in which to write and develop editing and rewriting skills, and the most active publish annual anthologies of their members' work.

Next, consider enrolling in a writing workshop. These are advertised in writers' newsletters and are offered by writers' centres, educational institutions and private tutors. Some are short-term and intensive (for example, a weekend), others long-term (for example, once a week for a year). Most workshops allocate time to formal instruction, group discussion and workshopping participants' manuscripts. Amy Tan's first novel, *The Joy Luck Club*, grew out of feedback on a short story that Tan had presented to a writers' workshop. However don't be surprised if few members of a writing group give consistently valuable advice. There's not much you can do with a comment like, 'I don't really like your main character'. What does it mean? Is it a personal reaction or a statement about writing craft? Is your main character under-developed, wasted, inconsistent?

Even though most published novels and stories are written without benefit of formal instruction, you might also consider enrolling in a degree or diploma writing course offered by a university or TAFE college. You can't assume that a course can train you to write or be a writer, however, for only years of solitary dedication can accomplish that, and don't become a 'professional student' of such courses as a way of avoiding writing. The best that a good writing teacher can do is stimulate, demonstrate and encourage you to teach yourself by getting you to place more demands upon yourself.

Be wary of correspondence courses, for these may be costly and you forgo the benefit of personal contact with professional writers and your peers.

The Internet provides many opportunities for writers seeking feedback on their work. Where writers once used the Internet mainly for gaining information, they can now also take part in on-line discussions, read the electronic versions of magazines and newspapers such as *overland* and *The New York Times Book Review*, submit their work to electronic magazines and book publishers, or publish their work on their own web-sites. This form of publishing has the potential to reach a large and international readership, and to create opportunity for lively—if not always well-informed—feedback.

Finally, you might consider paying a manuscript assessment service for a written report on your work, or apply to work with a mentor through a writers' organisation.

Ultimately, however, no amount of external feedback can substitute for developing and valuing your own sense of authority.

join the writing culture

Writing is a solitary activity. This suits most writers, and how else is a story or novel going to get written? But sometimes isolation can be crippling, and so you might consider taking part in the wider literary and writing culture. Many new writers attend readings in pubs, libraries, bookshops and other venues in order to meet other writers, gain a sense of what's being written, and find an outlet for their work. They also join writers' organisations—most of which offer workshops, public lectures, newsletters and information about short-story and poetry competitions—and regularly visit bookshops and read book reviews.

your first submission

Although getting into print involves the issues of finding a publisher, copyright and negotiating contracts (all of which lie outside the scope of this book) *state of mind* is also important. Once you have finished your final draft, selected an appropriate magazine or publishing house and submitted the manuscript, prepare to wait three or more months for a decision. Rather than sit chewing your nails, begin a new project at once. Identify your strengths and interests and follow these, and learn to identify opportunities. For example, I saw that my successful short story, 'The Bamboo Flute', which won an award and was published in a literary magazine, could be expanded and reworked as a novel for children. Since publication in that form it has sold tens of thousands of copies around the world and has never been out of print.

Don't expect to be published immediately, although this may happen. Most new writers, and even many established writers, either have their work rejected or are asked to revise it. A well-known literary quarterly might receive 5000 short stories each year, and publish no more than a dozen of them. A book publisher might be sent 5000 unsolicited manuscripts each year but accept less than ten of them. If your manuscript is rejected, try not to think that *you* have been rejected. It may be that the publisher's list is full for the next year or two, they've just published a story or novel much like yours, they're only accepting manuscripts submitted via an agent or by authors already on their list, they don't publish fiction. Perhaps your subject matter (for example, inner-urban grunge) is no longer fashionable, or your manuscript simply needs more work. You're unlikely to be given a detailed response; after all, it's not the job of a publisher or an editor to give feedback unless your manuscript has been accepted. Either read your manuscript again with a critical eye, or send it elsewhere. The now-famous Australian novelist Elizabeth Jolley once had thirty-nine rejections in one year. Mem Fox's children's book, *Possum Magic*, a worldwide best-seller, was rejected by ten publishers and underwent many rewrites before it was finally published.

Even so, writing can be a world of envy, disappointment and depression—for all writers.

alternatives to commercial publication

Novels and shorter works published on the Internet have the potential to attract large and diverse readerships. Internet publishing also offers alternative types and means of *authorship*: for example, the opportunity to co-write a story or novel with several other writers, interact with another's work (alter it, help write it, add to or subtract from it), or contribute to an ongoing 'serial'. Books published on compact disc offer video, sound and animation in addition to text and illustrations.

Or, at a more basic level, you might consider handing out broadsheets of your work, reciting on street corners or reading in pubs and on community radio.

Self-publishing is becoming popular, as more and more authors, frustrated in their attempts to be published by traditional means, or wanting greater control over subject matter, literary quality, design and layout, decide to pay for the printing, promotion, distribution and sale of their books.

But don't confuse self-publishing, in which the author makes informed decisions about all stages of the process, with *vanity* publishing, in which the author merely pays to be published. Vanity book publishers charge very high sums and give little, if any, attention to promotion and distribution—because they have already been paid. Bookshops are unlikely to stock vanity publications or reviewers to review them. There are also several unscrupulous publishers of 'world' anthologies of stories and verse in which authors are expected to pay to have their work published and to buy the volume in which it appears. There is no 'quality control' of vanity publications, no feedback by an informed editor, no way of knowing if you're writing poorly or well.

dealing with family and friends

When you begin writing regularly, certain changes will occur to your daily life. Some of them you'll bring about yourself; others will happen inevitably.

Your announcement that you intend to write will be greeted with mixed reactions from family and friends. If you're young you may be treated indulgently, or told there's no money in it (which is true), or told to get a good job first and write in your spare time. If you're retired, your writing may be viewed as a harmless way of passing the time. If you leave a good job to write, there may be frowns and recriminations. If you live with others, your insistence upon quietness, uninterrupted writing time, new equipment, a space in which to work, and a reallocation of domestic responsibilities might attract indifference, hostility or trade-offs. If you have little success early in your writing career the reaction might be: 'I told you so.' And you'll meet people who say, when you tell them that you're a writer, 'Yes, but what's your real job?' Writing is both undervalued and misunderstood.

Of course, those closest to you might also be understanding and supportive, recognising your need to write, helping you to create the best possible environment in which to write, and not forever judging your progress. You can return the favour by making compromises and not setting yourself up as a rare genius who must be tolerated and pampered. Value yourself and your work, but be prepared to learn, too, for a long apprenticeship is ahead of you.

two

WHAT IS FICTION?

Fiction is fact distorted into truth.
EDWARD ALBEE

I've often heard people say, 'I'm going to write a fiction novel'. Perhaps they understand 'novel' to mean 'book', for on the face of it the statement is tautological: a novel *is* fiction. It also implies that there could be such a thing as a *non*-fiction novel, which is absurd.

Or is it?

This chapter examines types of fiction, some reasons for fiction's enduring appeal, and the recent blurring between fiction and non-fiction.

THE CHANGING NATURE OF FICTION

storytelling

There has always been an oral tradition of storytelling. Humans quickly learned to embellish their bare reports of the day's events with fictional situations, characters and outcomes.

Myths, legends, folktales and fairytales grew out of these, as simple stories or as cautionary or instructive tales, often changing with the retelling, even when writing and printing were introduced.

forms of fiction

Over time the novel and the short story established themselves as the main forms of fiction, but there are many others, including the short novel, the novella, faction, hypertext novels and discontinuous narratives. We generally understand works of fiction to be *made up*—inventions of the author, in other words. They might be pure inventions, or speculations, or based to greater or lesser degrees on actual characters or events, but they are always *constructed* of certain formal features: character, point of view, narrative, symbolism, prose and theme, as discussed in later chapters.

In most stories and novels these features work together to create a harmonious whole but one feature will generally stand out more than the others. For example, in the F. Scott Fitzgerald novel, *The Great Gatsby*, point of view is emphasised. The story is told in the first-person point of view not by the main character, which we'd normally expect, but by Nick Carraway, a peripheral character, an observer. How does this skew the story? In the Conrad Aiken short story, 'Silent Snow, Secret Snow', the central image of snow stands out. At one level, the snow is real, but in its coldness and steady accumulation it also symbolises the gradual withdrawal from reality of the boy, Paul. In William Gass's short story, 'In the Heart of the Heart of the Country', structure dominates. The poet-narrator, a man 'in retirement from love', comments variously on the constrictions and frustrations of life in the American

Midwest under a series of headings such as 'My House', 'Vital Data' and 'Household Apples'.

the realist tradition

Most fiction is *realist* in the sense that, owing to the accumulation of detail, both the characters and the setting seem *real* to the reader. Realist fiction is strongly plotted, often around a meaningful theme such as 'loss of innocence', and the events are arranged chronologically to draw inexorably to a logical climax involving epiphanies for the main character, loose ends tied up, secrets revealed or mysteries solved. The world is complete and harmonious, and truths and values are universal. Readers are encouraged to suspend disbelief, to forget that an author is manipulating characters and events. Even in historical, science-fiction or fantasy stories and novels the characters and settings will seem realistic within their imagined contexts.

innovations

Writers have always departed from the realist tradition to greater or lesser degrees. Formal innovation over the past one hundred years has ranged from fiction becoming less concerned with plot than with character and atmosphere, to fiction that is mocking, parodic, ironical, self-referential, playful, irreverent and bizarre. Magical elements have been blended with the real, or narrative conventions dispensed with to suggest the arbitrariness and randomness of real life. Readers have been encouraged to read differently, help construct the work, or be reminded that it is a construction. Characters have been created as flat, unmotivated, even caricatured, so as to achieve a heightened or surreal effect. Themes have been dispensed with and the distinction between high and popular literary forms broken down.

blurring fiction and non-fiction

In recent years, influenced partly by Truman Capote's *In Cold Blood*—which is the 'novelisation' of a true crime—and other works of 'faction', there have been a number of books that blend fact and fiction or treat actual events and characters with the techniques of fiction. Here the Australian writer Arnold Zable discusses how the 'thin boundary between fiction and non-fiction' accounts for why his prize-winning work of non-fiction, *Jewels and Ashes*, is sometimes called a novel:

> *Jewels and Ashes* uses a number of 'fictional' devices. First, while the journey to Russia and Poland to trace my ancestors did take place, I reordered the sequence of certain events so that the book had added tension. I was concerned, as most writers are, to draw the reader along, and to keep them with me. Second, there are a number of composite characters which draw upon several people I have known. While I did this in order to hide the identity of actual people, I believe that this technique has enabled me to create more subtle portraits. Third, I recreate conversations which took place long before I was born. As I point out in the short author's note in *Jewels and Ashes*, while all place names and historical events were thoroughly researched, 'this is not primarily a work of history. Instead, it is concerned with the way in which family stories become, in time, ancestral legends. As the author recreating such stories, I am, of course, a part of the process'.

Zable goes on to discuss the importance of being selective; for example, he didn't record certain incidents of his childhood out of respect for his mother, who was still alive while he was writing *Jewels and Ashes*. At the same time, he was remaking and inventing, experiencing the liberation of a fiction writer:

> These are judgements which we must make when we sit at the writing desk. As writers we are, I think, motivated by a desire to explore the depths of the human experience, and to know ourselves and the world around us...Our lives...are far more wondrous and elusive than our wildest imaginings; they cannot be confined within strictly defined boundaries.

As an exercise, take a momentous incident or decision from your life and rewrite it as though it were happening to someone as unlike you as possible.

what's fashionable?

In fiction writing, as with other art forms, various approaches will always co-exist, but there will also be broad tendencies— such as the move away from the traditional realist model—and short-term trends—such as the popularity of 'dirty realism' in the 1970s and 1980s, in which American short-story writers like Raymond Carver and Bobbie Ann Mason wrote about the modest, easily-dashed dreams of the blue-collar characters who inhabit the diners, tract houses and taverns of small-town and regional America. Often these movements act as a breath of fresh air on fiction that has become staid or no longer 'speaks' to the majority of readers, but new writers should be wary of following a trend that won't last the distance or about which they know little. It's probably best to write something that only you can write.

labelling writers and writing

It became apparent in the latter half of the twentieth century that women, gay, lesbian, black and other writers had been sidelined or overlooked. One result of efforts to bring them in from the margins was the application of labels such as 'gay', 'black' and 'immigrant' writing; another was the introduction of specialist publishing houses or the publication of specialist lists or theme anthologies. Although many new writers and types of writing were thus brought to the attention of readers, the writers themselves now argue that they've been further marginalised, and should simply be known as 'a writer who happens to be Greek', for example, or 'a writer who happened to write a gay novel'.

WHAT SHOULD FICTION DO?

Tolstoy once dismissed Shakespeare on the grounds that he was 'not in earnest, but...playing with words'. The world of writing is full of prescriptions and judgements: for example, that short stories should have a twist in the tail; that men shouldn't write as women, or heterosexuals as gays, or whites as blacks; that there has to be a message; that novels should deal with important ideas or the big issues of the day; that fiction should bring about personal, moral or social change; that rural settings are inherently conservative as subjects for fiction; that X is a woman's book, Y is a man's book, and so on. Frank Lentricchia, an American teacher of literature, once heard a student attack the Don DeLillo novel, *White Noise*, for its insensitivity to the Third World. When Lentricchia pointed out that *White Noise* didn't concern the Third World but the technological catastrophes of the First World, the student responded, 'That's the problem. It's ethnocentric and elitist'.

It's easy to dismiss the opinions and positions outlined above, but what *should* fiction do? Or, to put it another way, why read it?

Rather than set out a list of prescriptions, I'll answer by saying what *I* look for in fiction—recognising that many of you will have, or develop, different expectations but also hoping that my position might help you clarify your own. Sometimes I enjoy reading about ideas, but mostly I read for the characters and the story. I like it that fiction can take me into familiar *and* unfamiliar worlds. Narrative is sometimes seen as unfashionable, but humankind's need for story, the desire to know what happens next, is undeniable. I like the beguilement in a puzzle, which obliges me to order and make sense of apparently random fragments of information as they accumulate. Heroes and anti-heroes appeal to me: I might recognise myself in them, or want to be like them, or love to hate them. They all have some excitement in their lives. I can't discount the vicarious pleasures of the car chase, the heart-stopping plot reversal, the threat of violence or steamy sex. I like writing that makes pictures in my head, so that I can taste the stale donut, smell the toxins in the air, feel the grit under my shoes. I enjoy reading good stylists, from the edgy, hyper James Ellroy to the Faulknerian Cormac McCarthy.

I like to laugh at sly asides, dark wit, wisecracks and the pungent observations of an unimpressed mind.

Good fiction also tells me things I didn't know, acts as a barometer of the community, or encourages me to imagine. Sometimes it reassures me, especially when it seems that random forces rule our lives and dishonesty and corruption win the day. I don't necessarily ask for a moral centre in fiction (although I know I'll get it in a good crime novel). I like to step inside the skin of someone who is not me, meet con-men, hustlers and low-lifes, and be taken somewhere I've never been before. Finally, I can acknowledge the darker side of myself, for without it I could not read—or write—fiction.

three

IDEAS FOR STORIES AND NOVELS

Look long and hard at the things that please you;
even longer and harder at what causes you pain.
COLETTE

'I don't know what to write about.'

'I have nothing to write about.'

'I'm just a housewife, nothing's ever happened to me.'

'I've got nothing to say.'

'I've got good ideas but don't know how to use them.'

'I can never come up with anything original or unique.'

Anxiety about ideas, their originality and developing them into works of fiction, are common in new—and even experienced—writers. As this chapter shows, the material for fiction is ever-present, need not be new and different, and can be developed in a number of ways.

FINDING IDEAS

Experienced writers find ideas for fiction in everything that's in and around them: dreams; unusual, humorous or moving newspaper items; snatches of overheard conversation; observations about people's mannerisms and relationships; anecdotes; character descriptions and profiles; speculations (asking the question, 'What if...?'); incidents they've witnessed; responses to books, films, paintings, music; painful or pleasing experiences; landscapes; plot outlines; beginnings; endings.

Sometimes writers start with an image. Sena Naslund, author of *Ahab's Wife*, was driving her car when she had a vision of a woman gazing out to sea, waiting for her husband. When Naslund heard the woman say, 'Captain Ahab was neither my first husband nor my last', she knew that she had her novel. Artefacts and documents, such as family photographs, letters and diaries, have also been the source of many stories and novels. Alex Miller's *Conditions of Faith* grew out of a journal kept by his mother when she was a young woman working in Paris in the 1920s. According to Miller:

> I'd lived in Paris for a time in the '70s and I could see my mother there, alone, filled with curiosity and a passion to live a full and rich life. I couldn't resist the invitation to write about her. It was like entering her secret life. Well, of course, Emily Stanton [Miller's main character] is not my mother...One always writes about oneself in the end.

Writers *notice*; they can't help it. Sometimes they find ideas when not looking for them (such as the sensation of released memory experienced by Proust when he tasted a madeleine dipped in tea), or find them serendipitously, or are reminded of things forgotten or deeply buried—but they know never to ignore them, even if the significance or meaning is not immediately apparent. They know that many of their ideas will never be used, while others will await their time; some will amount to no more than scenes, incidents or characters, while a handful will grow into stories and novels.

It's not uncommon for writers to sit on an idea for several years until another idea intersects with or complements it— until, in the words of Aristotle, they recognise 'the correspondence between things'. David Malouf has said that his novel, *Conversations at Curlow Creek*, grew out of two separate ideas

> that belonged to different works. One was the idea of a conversation between two people who are in something like the situation in the book [and the other was] about a man who is in love with a woman who is in love with someone else. I suddenly saw a way of matching the two...

Certain situations are popular because they have the potential for drama and conflict. For example, there are many works of fiction about mismatched people forced into one another's company by circumstances, or small communities that mirror the tensions of the wider community, or ordinary individuals responding to extraordinary stress, or the rise of one character's fortunes as another's fortunes fall. Many short stories are about a pair of characters (for example, lovers, a sister and her brother, a child and her favourite doll) whose relationship is tested or changed as a result of an intruding person or influence.

New writers are often advised: Write about what you know. I agree—up to a point. Certainly writing about familiar subjects and experiences can help diffident writers, but as Graham Swift said of his novel, *Ever After*, which deals with grief and loss, neither of which he'd experienced: 'Fiction is not writing about what you know, it's writing about things you don't have experience of. It's not about mirrors, it's about imagination.'

I think that confident writers should feel able to tackle the unknown: strange worlds, unfamiliar subjects and stepping inside the skins of strangers (backed by good research, of course). Nevertheless, we often write unwittingly about the things we know and understand *within* the framework of the unknown. For example, I might set out to write a prison novel—having never committed a crime or been imprisoned—and find that, in effect, I was writing about institutional life, bullying and being an outsider, of which I do have a little experience.

Most fiction writers use material from their own lives at some stage and to some degree, however. Some tell their own stories over and over again, others rarely. Experiences are central in the work of some writers, merely hinted at or heavily disguised in others. For example, to help create the voice and experiences of Paul, the twelve-year-old farm boy narrator of my novel, *The Bamboo Flute*, I was able to use the intense envy that I remembered feeling for the town kids when I'd been a twelve-year-old farm kid. In almost all other respects, Paul is not me but a character I've created.

A common mistake for new writers who draw on experiences is to report *what really happened*. The unmoved reader (a friend, a creative writing teacher, an editor) says politely, 'So what?' The writer insists, 'But all of these harrowing things really happened to me!'

The answer lies in an observation by the American poet John Ciardi: 'The act of writing a poem is not the act of having an emotion but the act of communicating it.' In other words, the writer's task is to encourage the reader to share, understand or sympathise with the emotion; that is, to 'touch' the reader in some way. Unless writers have a perspective on what really happened, their account of it will read like a report, not fiction. It will have none of the 'truth', universality or relevance of fiction. If you can look with a detached but perceptive and sympathetic eye upon a distressing event and say, for example, 'I behaved badly then', or 'I was very naïve in those days', then you are in a position to turn that event into fiction. Once you have identified the *point* of what really happened, you might find it useful to change the actual outcome, invent characters, delete characters, tell only part of the story, make a different character central to the story. It's common for fiction writers to treat actual events in this way. In fact, actual events become imagined ones as the imagination reshapes them.

I learned this with the first short story I'd ever attempted to write. Back in my student days I shared an old house with six other students. One night we went to a party together, crammed into an old car. We were thoroughly drunk by the time we left the party several hours later and were pulled over by a young policeman a few hundred metres short of home. To his credit the policeman was tactful, patient, amused, and prepared to let us drive home, but warned us not to drive again that night.

Then, without warning, someone in the back seat murmured, 'Pig.'

The policeman stiffened at the window and said, 'What did you say?'

The speaker, emboldened by drink, said loudly, *'Pig!'*

At once everything went wrong. We were ordered out of the car and the driver arrested. Back-up officers were called and we and the car were searched for drugs. There were no drugs, but we were being punished because one idiot had called the policeman a pig.

I was struck by the drama of that experience, the strong emotions, the sudden reversal in our fortunes, and set out to write about it. Twenty pages later I still hadn't got to the drive homeward: I'd got bogged down in characterising myself and the others, the house we lived in, and the party itself.

Later I realised several things: I didn't need the seven students or the sundry party animals. I could tell that same story quite well with only three characters: the policeman, the driver, and the driver's drunken mate. I also didn't need the student digs or the party; by concentrating on the interception in the street, and merely suggesting the rest, I was able to create a much more contained and dramatic situation. And I soon discovered that I was no longer writing about what really happened to me that night but creating characters and events based on what really happened.

IDEAS AND CHARACTERS

Your initial idea does not have to involve characters. It's not unusual for novels and stories to stem from images or clusters of images of landscapes or buildings, or from moods or atmospheres—from 'character-less' ideas, in other words. But until you have characters you'll find it hard to move far beyond that starting point.

The novelist Liam Davison has said: 'Each of my novels has started with a particular location...and the strangely numinous quality it has for me', but adds: 'and a sense of wonder or intrigue about the stories it carries.' In those stories he finds his characters.

WRITING TRIGGERS

Almost anything can trigger a mood, memory or idea that leads to writing a story or novel. The following exercises may help get you started.

1. Write a list of words and images in response to a photograph, painting or piece of classical music, and develop the most promising or appealing.
2. Look at a tennis ball. Describe it, and its function, in plain, neutral language, then relate a tennis-ball incident from your childhood.
3. Describe a derelict house in the country in terms of: an old man returning to his childhood home; squatters discovering that it's haunted; yuppies who have inherited it in a will.
4. Take an everyday homily, such as 'Pride comes before a fall', and write a real or imagined story to illustrate it.
5. Use one of these first lines of existing short stories to write your own story: 'Theo had a choice between a drug that would save his sight and a drug that would keep him alive, so he chose not to go blind' (David Leavitt). 'I know what is being said about me and you can take my side or theirs, that's your own business' (Truman Capote).
6. Cinnamon. Brainstorm it (colour, function, odour, a memory, appearance, the spice trade, a shop, a meal...)
7. Write an evocative account of touching a balloon or a feather. When did you last touch a feather or a balloon? When did you first touch one? Describe your feelings then.

8. We've all seen a stranger in tears, on a street or in a railway carriage. Write about the incident or memory that might have caused the stranger to cry.

THE SCOPE OF YOUR IDEA

That sentence or phrase scribbled in your notebook: how substantial is it? Is it the basis for a novel? A short story? Or something more modest, such as a scene or a character?

During the past fifteen years I have abandoned four novels for various reasons. I'm reluctant to throw anything away, however, and reworked two of them successfully as short stories and the other two as shorter novels. As a result I'm now convinced that I'd been over-reaching each time, that the four ideas hadn't the potential to work as novels, just as I'm convinced that many of the novels I read are excessively padded-out short stories.

It's important to consider the scale of your ideas before and during the writing process, especially as their apparent potential may not be realised. Some ideas are clearly the basis for novels, others are harder to gauge. Many of my ideas are sentences or phrases scribbled onto scraps of paper and shoved into my 'ideas' folders. One day I came across this note: *the anxious, obsessive man in the internment camp*, and immediately saw the broad outlines of a novel in my head. I had made the note many years earlier, when, during research for a history textbook, I'd discovered a collection of letters by German and Italian immigrants who'd been interned as a security risk during the Second World War. The note reminded me of the heartache in their voices, and at once I sat down to write the story of one such man.

As an exercise, examine the following situations and then gauge which has the potential to be a short story and which a novel.

1. Jade, fabulously beautiful, is born on the wrong side of town. A heroin addict at fifteen and a prostitute at sixteen, she later kicks her habit and remakes herself as a high-priced call-girl. When she's eighteen she marries one of her clients, a wealthy widower who has twin sons and owns a cosmetics firm. A couple of years later, her husband dies in mysterious circumstances and she's now head of the cosmetics firm. Clever and ruthless, she soon builds it into an empire with offices in London, Paris and New York. She has affairs with racing-car drivers, popstars and Hollywood actors. The years go by. One day, when she's in her fifties, the twins gang up on her and try to force her out...

2. Ed, Justin and Stefan are school mates, fifteen years old, bored and restless. As they leave the cinema one Friday evening, they notice an unlocked car with the keys in the ignition. 'Let's steal it,' Ed says. 'Okay,' says Justin. 'Not a good idea,' says Stefan. Ed and Justin begin to gang up on Stefan, calling him names, goading him, accusing him of cowardice. Stefan walks home, thinking that he should have got into the car with the others, knowing that he'll be the butt of their cruel teasing at school on Monday morning. But when Monday comes he learns that Ed and Justin had crashed the car and been killed (or horribly disfigured). Now he's filled with conflicting emotions: 'If only I'd tried harder to talk them out of it,' and, 'Thank God I didn't get into the car with them.'

Could you do justice to the first example in a ten-page short story? No—you'd barely cover the basic storyline, let alone bring scenes or characters to life. The busy plot, time frame, setting changes and large cast demand several hundred pages—a novel, in fact.

The more contained situation of the second example is best suited to the short-story form (see Chapter 11). This is not to say that it could not be developed as a novel, but the novel would be both denser and broader than the outline given above.

INVEST IN YOUR IDEA

Readers—including fiction editors—are quick to notice a writer's lack of engagement with his or her material. If you're bored, intent on making a quick buck or choosing subjects you think will impress an editor, it's bound to show in the tone and style of your work.

It pays to ask yourself: 'Is this idea worth the effort?' and 'Do I have a pressing need to explore this idea?' The story or novel that has a necessity for the writer, that comes as a surprise and works through the disclosure of what is painful and intimate, will always seem strong, 'authentic' and heartfelt to the reader.

THE SIGNIFICANT AND THE MUNDANE

New writers often believe that fiction should deal only with matters of great substance and impact: be inspired by profound or original ideas, for example, or about important issues, or peopled with characters spouting great notions, or full of headlong action. In fact, some of the best and most successful and enduring stories and novels deal with humble themes and everyday events and characters. The writer's task lies in making these *seem* significant, not only for the characters involved but also for the reader. Richard Ford's short novel, *Wildlife*, about the modest hopes and disappointments of ordinary people, is far more devastating than the latest blockbuster dealing with a terrorist attack on the United States. Situations aren't trite and dull, authors or their words are.

'But I have lived a humdrum life,' you say. 'Nothing has happened to me.'

I'd rather read a fresh, honest, unflinching story about an old man with only five dollars in his pocket until pension day than a clichéd story about the American president trying to avert a world war. As Flannery O'Connor has said, writers are set up for life by childhood and adolescence. By adulthood we know something about love, hatred, envy, jealousy, fear, desire or any of the other great subjects of literature. In other words, write about what genuinely interests you rather than what you feel you *should be* interested in. What themes, questions or situations preoccupy you most?

NEW, UNIQUE, DIFFERENT

New writers also think that it's wrong to tackle subjects that have been written about before. In some circumstances this can be wise advice, given that literary trends are often shortlived (for example, the glut of inner-city, sex-and-heroin, grunge novels in the mid-1990s), but publishers (and readers) will always value a fresh approach to an old subject. It's better to look for the truth about who we are and what life means than look for something new; what matters is not that you've written another boy-meets-girl novel but *how* you've written it. In fact, recurring themes and ideas mark the fiction of many prominent writers—and it's been said that there are only seven basic plots in fiction: boy meets girl; crime and punishment; the worm turns; the eternal triangle; revenge; the quest; and slaying the dragon. If these are told freshly and honestly, they will seem fresh and honest, and therefore *original,* to the reader.

DEVELOPING IDEAS

Often your idea will be no more than a word, a phrase, or one or two dashed-off sentences in your notebook. You're a long way short of a character or scene, let alone a short story or novel. Experienced writers will take an idea and begin to poke at it with appropriate questions; for example: What if X happened instead? What happened before this? What might happen next? Who loses, who wins? Who has most at stake? What is her motivation? What is holding him back?

In much the same way that a pearl is formed as a coating around an irritant, writers can allow an idea to accrue material until it has substance. Writing fiction often requires this kind of persistence, together with a narrow focus. Learn patience. I have sometimes waited years before developing certain ideas into stories or novels. In some cases I'd lacked wisdom, knowledge or experience; in others I was waiting for further ideas to intersect with or complete the initial ones.

Some writers start with a certain atmosphere and then find the characters and actions to express and develop it. Other writers start with a situation and a character and write to see what will happen, for writing is often a process of discovery, of uncovering things you didn't know you knew, felt or believed. When Flannery O'Connor started her story 'Good Country People' she found herself writing a description of two women and equipping one of them with a daughter with a wooden leg. She then found herself introducing a Bible salesman, but didn't know that he was going to steal the wooden leg until a few lines before he did it. By then, O'Connor said, it seemed inevitable. Raymond Carver once began a short story of which he knew only the first line. Gradually the second sentence and then the third attached themselves, until eventually he could see his story. Graham Swift has said:

> The worst thing you can do is force a novel into being. Now I just wait for them to happen. My novels don't tend to begin with a good idea, they start with a little scene or a situation. With *Waterland*, the scene was a body in a river—a cliché, but in a specific landscape which provided the context for the story. In *Out of This World*, a boy discovers a photograph of a woman and knows it is his mother. With *Ever After*, Bill Unwin, the narrator, sees a group of ballet students through a window in Paris—that is what I begin with.

Many writers see the novel as a long meditation, a gradual process of evolution, in which story and character are discovered during the exploration of half-formed and apparently unconnected notions. Rodney Hall's novel *Just Relations* began with notes that Hall made about a country-town shop with its 'rather strange old lady' proprietor and rows of dusty gumboots. Then in another such shop he heard a young man ask for 'a stick of gelignite to blow up a bullock'. Hall put the two images together and began to explore threads of implication, as though starting from 'the middle of a giant spider's web'. After 70000 words he realised that he was writing a novel, not a sketch, and let its plot evolve as he wrote.

Some stories and novels will require research. I spoke to detectives before writing my crime novel, *The Dragon Man*, for example, and read library and archival material for my novel of the Second World War, *Past the Headlands*. I love research. At times it's systematic, at other times it involves random leads, side tracks, suppositions, lucky finds and dead ends.

When dealing with a mass of material, learn the arts of *selection* (for example, write about a key or representative day of a holiday romance rather than a string of days and experiences) and *specification* (focusing on single moments, emotions or incidents).

Remember that a seemingly flawless novel or short story is bound to have gone through a number of discarded ideas, direction changes and messy drafts.

IDEAS AND THEME

You tell a friend that you've written a novel. She asks what it's about. You find yourself unable to give a succinct answer.

Even experienced writers face this problem from time to time. It can be helpful to think about the distinction between theme, plot and storyline. For example, the *theme* of Colette's classic short story, 'The Other Wife', is 'loss of innocence'. The *plot* is 'When a young, newly-married woman discovers feet of clay in her older, recently divorced husband, she begins to question her marriage to him'. The *storyline* is 'One day Marc and Alice are driven by their chauffeur to a restaurant for lunch. Just as they are about to be seated, Marc notices the presence of his ex-wife in the restaurant. He quickly steers Alice to a different table and...'

Most stories and novels make a point or express a theme through the arrangement of events. Sometimes the theme may be found in the opening sentence—the classic example of this is Tolstoy's *Anna Karenina*: 'All families are alike but an unhappy family is unhappy after its own fashion.' Writers often don't know what the theme is when they begin to write, however, but once identified, it can help them rewrite or avoid unprofitable diversions. The theme is generally related to the central conflict, and can often be summed up in a phrase or sentence, for example: 'love conquers all', 'the getting of wisdom', 'we always hurt the ones we love', 'pride comes before a fall', 'with success comes dissatisfaction'. In fact, many stories and novels boil down to the theme of characters searching for a true home. Theme need not be dramatic or profound but may simply express an aspect of human nature. At the same time, writers might want to bear in mind Chekhov's belief that it is the role of artists to pose questions, not answer them.

four

CHARACTER

> *I have never started from ideas but*
> *always from character.*
> TURGENEV

I believe that character is the central element of fiction writing. Characters help fiction writers enter, tell and shape their novels and stories, express ideas, and drive and develop plots.

TYPES OF CHARACTERS

Novels and stories will have all or some of the following: the main character (there may be more than one); the 'goals' of the main character (for example, a potential lover); those who help the main character; those who hinder the main character; and those who influence the main character in passing.

You will generally know who the main character is at the start, but sometimes this isn't clear, or you will discover, as you write, that one of the minor characters would make a better main character. If in doubt, try asking: Who has most at stake? Who is most often at centre stage? Who is the most active agent? Who is telling the story? And simply, whom do you like best? With whom do you empathise?

Learn to be flexible, to accommodate your characters as they live and grow in your imagination. As you know more about the characters and the story, you might, as the American crime writer Elmore Leonard does, turn the spotlight from one character onto another. You might also choose apparently unlikely main characters: for example, the hired killer in Lawrence Block's novel, *Hit Man*.

Novels and stories also have minor characters. These may be viewed as having a specific function, such as giving information through dialogue at a key stage of the story, but I've often found that inexperienced writers introduce far more characters than a story needs. While these 'bit parts' can add colour and movement, they also slow the action, clutter the foreground and confuse the reader. As you review and edit your work, you may well find yourself cutting out superfluous characters, or making it clear—by not naming or developing them—that they are merely 'extras' who will disappear.

Even so, minor characters need to be believable, not props or stereotypes. While generally not as developed in their complexity as the main characters, they can be made vivid on the page quickly by means of a particular physical tag, manner of speaking, personality trait or name. Evoking their relationships to the main character helps flesh both out.

CHARACTER AS A PLOTTING AID

The English novelist John Galsworthy said that 'character is plot'. A plot is advanced as we advance into characters: as characters reflect, make decisions, act, react, intrigue with and manoeuvre against one another, so a plot unfolds. It therefore helps fiction writers if they understand their characters well. The result is easier plotting, characters who are believable on the page, and actions that are explicable to the reader (even if not immediately so). Characters who seem vague, static or contradictory to the writer will also appear that way to the reader, and lead the writer into plot difficulties.

It helps to have some idea of your characters before you begin, but it's not unusual for writers to learn about their characters as they write. Anne Tyler said of the narrator of her novel, *A Patchwork Planet*:

> I had trouble at first getting Barnaby to 'open up' to me—
> he was...thorny and difficult...and we had a sort of sparring,
> tussling relationship until I grew more familiar with him.

Characters influence plot in many ways, and motivation is the key. Even if you have created interesting characters they won't assist with plot development unless they face challenging situations that compel them to act, or arouse an emotional response. What do they want? What do they need? What do they fear? What risks are they prepared to take to achieve their aims? A character's path of action should ultimately seem plausible and inevitable, given their personality and circumstances.

Even when you have a solid grasp of the plot and are well advanced with the writing, your characters might still force you into a reassessment of it. I'd intended my novel, *The Stencil Man*, about a German–Australian man interned as a security risk during the Second World War, to be a 'prison' novel. I felt that I had a thorough knowledge of the main character, his situation and the world of the internment camp, but then, several months and many thousands of words later, a niggling idea entered my head: 'Martin's going to escape.' I stopped writing for some time and took long walks, examining the pros and cons of Martin's escaping from the camp. It all boiled down to his character. I asked myself: Why does he want to escape? Is it something he desires, or is he being pushed, or both? *Would* he take such a risk, given the sort of man he is? Has he changed? Certainly the escape opened up the novel and gave it a shot of energy, but I didn't *impose* it onto the existing plot for the sake of entertaining the reader; rather, it grew naturally out of what I'd already established.

CHARACTER AND CONFLICT

Characters in stories and novels usually have some kind of problem to solve, arising out of or compounded by certain types of conflict. These are: inner conflict (for example, a character must overcome shyness if she is to achieve a certain goal); conflict with nature (a character battling a blizzard in an adventure story); conflict with other characters (a rival in love); and conflict with society's values (a young man from a bigoted Protestant family falls in love with a young woman from a Catholic family). Note that one type of conflict is likely to be bound up with others, resulting in story density and complexity. For example, our young Protestant man might have to overcome shyness, a rival lover *and* the bigotry of his family.

Your characters may be in a state of psychological stress as a result of conflict, which, in turn, offers opportunities for you to draw them as complex rather than predictable beings. They might ultimately make the 'right' decision but, in the process, deceive themselves, rationalise the problem, blame others or become apathetic, depressed or erratic. And failure to achieve their goals might lead them to take on extreme views to mask their own, or to become successful in other activities as a compensation.

CHARACTER AND CLIMAX

As you balance the demands of plot and character, try to let your characters find their own solutions to problems. Yours is the controlling hand, of course, but if you know your characters well enough they will lead you to a solution that is true to their personalities and motivations, not one that is merely convenient to the plot. If the only solution you can find to a character's financial problems is to let him win a million dollars, it may be that you don't know him well enough. Such an ending will seem contrived to readers, a 'cop-out', one that side-steps character development and wastes all that has led up to it. Certainly a lottery windfall or a car accident can happen at just the right or wrong moment in real life, but they are unsatisfactory climaxes for fiction.

CHARACTER IS ACTION

Characters are active agents in fiction. No one wants to read a novel or story in which the main character never does anything. This doesn't mean that he or she must rob a bank or take a lover; even the movement of thoughts and feelings can give a sense of character movement, as we see in the 'interior' novels of Thomas Bernhard.

characters desire things

By acting on a desire, fictional characters may cause changes or repercussions for themselves and others. This may be true even if they *fail* to act (blocked by a character trait, or some external factor, for example). And so the story moves on.

characters want to preserve or to change the status quo

The status quo might be a relationship, a possession, a cherished notion or anything else a character might defend.

characters respond to other characters

When characters fall in love, sack an employee, punch a friend on the nose or sink into depression, their actions have consequences, for themselves and for others. Characters might also unwittingly have an impact on others simply because they pose a threat or represent authority.

characters make mistakes

How boring a novel or story would be if the hero never made mistakes. Mistakes rebound upon the hero, and for the reader there is a rise in tension and suspense.

characters face dilemmas

In a skilfully written novel or story, the reader can't help but be involved when characters are forced to decide between two equally compelling or undesirable courses of action.

characters come under stress

There will be times when your characters are faced with new, unfamiliar or taxing situations such as danger, the death of a loved one, the loss of a job. How will they respond? Perhaps an otherwise strong character will cave in under the pressure, or a weak character gain strength.

REVEALING CHARACTER

In most fiction it's the writer's task to persuade the reader that fictional characters are real, alive and worth responding to. Characterisation can be achieved in the following ways, but any one method will not be adequate by itself. A good writer will exploit various approaches to give as much information as possible.

Just as it takes time to get to know someone in real life, the same should apply to fictional characters. Remember not to reveal all aspects of character at once. Looks, mannerisms or particular responses to a situation can be effective ways of introducing a character. Subtleties can be revealed later, although they may be implied at the start. Try repeating and elaborating upon important features: for example, if a character is wearing a hearing aid when first introduced, he or she might later appear as isolated or withdrawn at a noisy dinner party.

motivation

We often speak of what makes people 'tick'—what they want, what they think and feel, why they act in certain ways, why they did X instead of Y: what *motivates* them, in other words. In short stories, characters usually have a central trait, such as shyness or a jealous nature, that influences the directions of their decisions. Characters in novels tend to have greater complexity and we may see a range of motives and actions. It can be useful for the sake of creating tension and suspense to hide, or delay revealing, the motive behind an act, but readers will be frustrated if it's never made explicable. Sometimes too, characters act out of character. The natures of fictional characters should be flexible, capable of changing, gaining in maturity and responding unexpectedly—as people do. Their actions should ultimately seem believable, however, rather than convenient short cuts to move the plot along.

show, don't tell

Describing rather than *evoking* is perhaps the most common error of beginner writers. A short, vivid scene (with speech and action) is worth pages of dry description. For example, when establishing that your main character is being physically abused at work, reinforce the point with an actual incident so that readers can see the bully's covert punch and hear the victim's pleading voice.

exposition

Another common failing is fiction writing in which characters are explained and interpreted in detail; that is, *told about* rather than *shown*. Consequently there is little room for a reader to speculate about a character's personality or motivation. This method is used in nineteenth-century novels like those of Charles Dickens (in which the plot structure, with its surprising turns and revelations, compensates) and modern blockbuster novels like those of Tom Clancy (in which the sweep of action compensates).

Writers can't always avoid passages of exposition, especially in novels, but it's a form best suited to non-fiction. Dramatic forms—showing characters speaking and acting—are, in fiction writing, much more effective in engaging readers.

description

A good writer won't give an exhaustive description but will reveal certain aspects of a character in a certain way and thereby *imply* his or her appearance and personality. Remember that external details can imply the inner person; for example, a man who pulls his tie into a tight knot at his neck might be mean or repressed.

Appearance alone is rarely adequate, however; it works best when supported by actions, thoughts, dialogue or the speculations of other characters. In this example, from Tim Winton's novel, *The Riders*, the main character, Scully, meets an Irish postman for the first time; note that the viewpoint is not neutral but filtered to us through Scully:

The driver killed the motor and opened the door.

'Jaysus,' said a long, freckled shambles of a man unfolding himself like a piece of worn patio furniture. 'I thought it was the truth all along.'

Beneath the postman's crumpled cap was a mob of red hair and two huge ears. Scully stood there anxiously.

'So there's someone livin back in Binchy's Bothy.'

'That's right,' said Scully. 'My third day.'

'Peter Keneally. They call me Pete-the-Post.'

Scully reached out and shook his freckled hand. 'G'day.'

The postie laughed, showing a terrible complement of teeth.

'Would you be Mister F. M. Scully, now?'

In the famous introduction to *Emma*, notice how Jane Austen has combined appearance, personality traits and social background:

Emma Woodhouse, handsome, clever and rich, with a comfortable home and happy disposition, seemed to unite some of the best blessings of existence; and had lived nearly twenty-one years in the world with very little to distress or vex her.

New writers often have to 'unlearn' the tendency to describe characters in clichéd terms. A character with 'long blonde hair and clear blue eyes' is as lifeless and featureless as a child's doll. And how many sailors have you met who walk 'with a rolling gait'? Try to be vivid and evocative, as in this (the only) description of a minor character in an American crime novel:

Shooter looked me over with heavy-lidded eyes in a face the colour of blue coal. He was a long trickle of water with bones showing under his skin in a tank top, striped shorts and sockless shoes. (Loren Estleman, *Silent Thunder*)

But not all novels and short stories provide much in the way of character description. Instead, readers form their own impressions from other aspects of the characters. According to the English novelist Julian Barnes:

I think...today's readers like to make their own picture of a character, and if you have got a sort of moral description of the person you only need to hint at the physical description.

behaviour

Actions reveal character, and characters reveal themselves in their actions. Characters can express through 'body language' not only permanent character traits, such as arrogance, but also responses to particular situations, such as sorrow at the death of a loved one. What can you surmise about the mood and personality of the commandant in the following passage?

> When the internees returned from their outing, the camp commandant was waiting for them on his office verandah in the military compound. He was smiling like a solicitous uncle. He knocked his pipe bowl against a verandah post and hurried down the steps, crying, 'Welcome back, welcome back. How did it go?'
>
> Dr Oser and Lieutenant Dinham met him as he crossed the yard, shook his hand, and in low voices told him about the riot in Tatura.
>
> 'Oh dear,' said the commandant. 'Oh dear, oh dear, oh dear.'
>
> After a while he walked among the internees, his empty pipe in his teeth, apologising, asking them if they were all right, asking if they had enjoyed the picnic at least. 'Yes,' they said. 'Thank you.' He said 'Dreadful' once or twice and got in the way when they unloaded the lorries.
>
> (Garry Disher, *The Stencil Man*)

dialogue

The words that fictional characters use, and the ways in which they are spoken, can reveal emotions and personality traits. Read the following extract. What sort of person is Kim in general? What mood is he in at this moment?

At the end of the year there was a school concert. They drove to the hall in Kim's car, and as he was backing into a parking spot between a concrete pillar and a brick wall, Sue turned around to Louise in the back seat and said, 'My clever girl.'

Louise's voice shook. 'Mum, I've forgotten the words.'

'No you haven't, my darling. You'll remember them when you're on the stage.'

Louise squealed, *'I've forgotten the words!'*

Kim jerked, scraping the car against the post. 'Bloody hell, look what you made me do.'

He stopped the car without completing the manoeuvre, letting the engine run. They sat there. After a while Sue touched his knee. 'Um, I'll get out and have a look, shall I?'

'I'm going home.' He got out his wallet. 'You can take a taxi after.'

'But you promised. Louise's first solo.'

'Oh, bloody Jesus Christ. Bloody Jesus Christ.' He yanked on the wheel, shot the car into another parking spot and walked apart from them into the hall.

(Garry Disher, 'Chain')

characters as they see themselves

Novelists and short-story writers often find it useful to show characters assessing themselves. But should we believe them? Are they reliable witnesses, in other words? Generally yes, but you might like to write a story or novel in which characters have a false or idealised image of themselves. A great example is Vladimir Nabokov's novel *Lolita*, in which the character Humbert Humbert tries to justify himself morally for seducing the twelve-year-old Lolita, but fails, and finally knows it. An interesting tension results when there is a discrepancy between what readers know about fictional characters and how those characters see themselves.

characters as seen by others

As people do in real life, fictional characters will judge, assess and respond to one another, and offer contrasting opinions of an individual according to their different viewpoints. In a first-person novel like *The Great Gatsby*, readers gain their impressions of Gatsby from many sources: the observations of the narrator, Nick Carraway; what Gatsby says about himself to Nick; what Daisy says to Nick about Gatsby; and in hearsay from other sources.

characters and settings

Characters are also informed by the settings in which they are placed (see Chapter 10). The use of an appropriate setting works well to round out a character—for example, a farmer on a farm or a tarot reader in a New Age community. A foreign or unfamiliar setting, with which the character is at odds, can also be effective—for example, a university student from a rural background trying to come to terms with life in a big city.

BELIEVABILITY

Beginner writers often ask how they can make fictional characters believable. The answer lies in letting them 'live and grow in your imagination exactly as if you saw them in the flesh' (Katherine Anne Porter). You need to be perceptive, wise, sympathetic and forgiving to be a writer, for you will be writing about good and bad characters, or qualities of goodness and badness, or qualities difficult to judge. I can't teach you how to be wise and understanding—how to develop the deep layering of a character, in other words—but the following examples may help illustrate ways you might develop your powers of observation and selection, and convey what is distinctive as well as everyday about your fictional characters:

- mannerisms: characters might sniff a lot, jingle the coins in their pockets, chew their nails, consistently look at their reflections in a mirror
- speech habits: swearing; using outmoded expressions; failing to finish sentences
- character traits: cynical; arrogant; inclined to apologise all the time
- attitudes and beliefs: racist; bigoted; fond of spouting little homilies about life
- strengths: a kind and loyal friend; will stand up to bullies
- weaknesses: always trying to please everybody; continually falling in love with the wrong type; apt to tell little white lies when under pressure.

names

Many writers find that they can't begin a story or novel until they know the names of their characters. Some names seem to fit certain character types; for example, I once created a jolly character called Sally, but had to change her name when she became a darker, more complex character. If I were creating a tough private eye, I wouldn't call him Wilbur Sidebottom. And an editor once red-pencilled my manuscript with the observation: 'Do you realise that all of your characters have forgettable, two-syllable Anglo-Saxon names like Johnson and Turner?' I've never forgotten that lesson.

tags

An aspect of appearance or behaviour can, if repeated, 'tag' or identify a character. This might take the form of a mannerism or speech habit (see above).

In other words, don't give readers the bland public face of a character. At the same time, remember that personality should be a *critical* instrument in fiction, not a mere list of contingencies and attributes, and that it is best viewed as a glimpse rather than full-on and all spelt out. Avoid stereotypes, too. There have been too many 'plodding policemen', 'spinster librarians' and 'dumb blondes' in fiction. Even if you intend to use a spinster librarian in a story or novel there should be more than that to say about her. Some fictional characters might be a symbol of something more, such as goodness or evil, but they should still be individuals; you don't want your readers saying that a character is too good or too evil to be true.

CHARACTER AND CONSISTENCY

You might find that your characters grow and change as you write, so that their actions and beliefs on page 200 are inconsistent with their actions and beliefs on page 10. Careful writers can solve this in the drafting stages, but what of characters who are *meant* to grow and change? A middle-aged housewife might well become a belly dancer in real life, but there will be convincing reasons for it, just as there should be for your fictional housewife. Try to get into the habit of testing your characters' motives and actions against what you know of their personalities, and try not to manipulate them to suit the plot but let them determine their own fates.

Bear in mind that behaviour might vary according to circumstances but still be consistent. In Jennifer Johnston's novel, *The Old Jest*, the main character behaves in different ways with different people as determined by the type of relationship she has with each.

It is usually best to reveal characteristics a little at a time, ensuring that you're painting a reasonably consistent picture so that readers don't find themselves making too many reassessments. However, try not to omit essential information about a character (or anything else) in the early part of a story or novel.

BASING FICTIONAL CHARACTERS ON REAL PEOPLE

Most novelists and short-story writers base their fictional characters on real people to a certain degree or at certain times. We have to start somewhere, and that's generally with ourselves and the people around us. Some writers rework aspects of their lives imaginatively, others graft imagined characters, settings and incidents onto actual experiences, and most take note of the habits and mannerisms of the people around them. We might observe that a friend begins projects enthusiastically but never completes them, for example, or that another bites the insides of her cheeks when she's tense. Sometimes we combine the characteristics of more than one actual person, if we can integrate them plausibly in the nature of the character.

In the act of setting such characters to work on the page, however, we tend to find that we're in fact *creating* characters rather than simply reporting real ones. When I started writing *The Bamboo Flute*, the narrator Paul, a twelve-year-old farm boy in the time of the Great Depression of the 1930s, was an amalgam of my father and myself, but as I wrote, Paul became a fully-rounded character in his own right, so that I saw and heard a fictional character in my mind's eye, not my father or my childhood self.

Writers also take historical figures and either recreate them or use them as the basis of fictional characters. At the centre of Pat Barker's novel, *Regeneration*, is a real-life encounter in 1917 between W. H. R. Rivers, an army psychologist, and the poet Siegfried Sassoon. Ron Hansen's *Hitler's Niece* evokes the relationship between Adolf Hitler and the daughter of his half-sister. The war photographer in Christopher Koch's *Highways to War* is based in part on the late Neil Davis. Other characters in each of these novels never existed in real life.

It can also be an effective device to use a *fringe* historical figure. The main character in Roger McDonald's novel, *Mr Darwin's Shooter*, is Syms Covington, Charles Darwin's manservant. Covington takes us into worlds (for example, life between decks on a nineteenth-century sailing ship) that would have been denied to us if Darwin had been the central character.

Finally, consider your legal and moral responsibilities when you base your fictional characters on living people. It can't be denied that writers sometimes feel vengeful, and gain satisfaction from exaggerating, deriding or destroying a fictional character who resembles someone who has done them wrong. In doing so recognisably, however, writers may expose themselves to charges of defamation. Even if what they wrote is the 'truth', as they see it, truth may not be a defence in defamation actions.

In terms of moral responsibilities, your best friend probably won't sue you for using her well-known penchant for all things French to characterise the main protagonist in your latest novel, but can you risk hurting her or losing her friendship?

If in doubt, seek legal advice and alert your publisher.

five

DIALOGUE

It begins with a character, usually, and once he stands up on his feet and begins to move, all I do is trot along behind him with a paper and pencil trying to keep up long enough to put down what he says and does.

WILLIAM FAULKNER

Dialogue is direct speech between fictional characters. It is used to characterise people, dramatise important scenes, provide information, and quicken reader interest. It helps to advance the plot, and provides verisimilitude—an air of being true to life. In fiction, as in life, characters will argue, be evasive, gossip and express their feelings. Many successful stories have been written without dialogue, but, if carefully exploited, dialogue is a useful tool for a writer. The J. D. Salinger story, 'Pretty Mouth and Green My Eyes', and the Paul Bailey novel, *At the Jerusalem*, are told almost entirely in dialogue, and yet it's used so skilfully that readers gain a convincing mental picture of characters and setting. First-person novels and stories (see Chapter 6) are also told through dialogue in the sense that the narrator, a character in the story, speaks directly to the reader, expressing hopes, fears, moods and personality traits.

DIALOGUE AND CHARACTERISATION

In real life we discover or surmise things about people as we listen to them. We pay attention not only to *who* is speaking but also to *what* is said, the *way* it is said, and *why*, and come to conclusions about the speaker's background and personality. In the same way, readers learn something about fictional characters.

Imagine that you are a fly on the wall in this scene: A boy at an exclusive private school has been bullying other boys and the headmaster has called the boy's parents into his office. The father, a self-made businessman, is irritated that he should be called to the school and he's convinced that his son isn't a bully. The mother sits quietly with her head bowed. Eventually, in the face of the headmaster's urbane, unimpressed manner, the father gets to his feet and snarls, 'Listen, Sunshine, you reckon I'd be what I am today if I hadn't learned to stand on me own two feet?' whereupon his wife murmurs, 'And what exactly *are* you today, dear?'

As you can see, many factors affect the dialogue in this scene. Not only is something different at stake for each character (that is, they each desire a different outcome), they are also speaking and acting according to their personalities in general *and* their moods on this particular occasion. At the moment, the above scene is a *report*. Try fleshing it out with more action and dialogue, paying attention to the hidden factors that seem to be emerging; for example, the headmaster despises self-made men even as he relies upon them for donations to the school; a widening rift develops between husband and wife; the husband's wealth and bluster can't hide the fact that he feels self-conscious about his lack of an education.

In order to make their characters sound convincing on the page, novelists and short-story writers try to know them well, listening to the moods they're in, recognising their personality traits and understanding how they'll respond in particular situations. Furthermore, they appreciate that speech can be a very subtle indicator of the formative backgrounds of their characters, even if these characters have moved on or up in the world, like our self-made businessman.

social class

An upper-class background might be revealed in an assured, educated, complacent tone, but remember that a working-class person might mask his roots by adopting upper-class inflexions.

age

A seventy-year-old grandmother probably won't talk about the 'cool time' she had last night, whereas her teenage granddaughter might. Then again, in an effort to appear up-to-date or to please her granddaughter, the grandmother might use teenage slang. Note too, that slang and colloquial expressions tend to date quickly, and are specific to certain historical periods. For example, the expression 'it's a hassle' will one day disappear, and didn't exist before the latter part of the twentieth century.

culture of origin

An American will use different slang, and some words differently, from an Australian or a Briton. Exaggerated or stereotypical accents are often distracting and difficult to read however, and may seem patronising. It's better to *suggest* an accent than try to mimic it exactly; for example, a man for whom English is a second language might structure his sentences idiosyncratically, or speak very stiffly or correctly, as does Keller, the Austrian-born piano teacher in Peter Goldsworthy's novel, *Maestro*.

level of education

A good education doesn't necessarily point to intelligence, but a well-educated person will probably use more complex sentences and words than someone who is not well educated.

life experiences

A woman who has had an unhappy marriage might speak cynically of men and marriage, for example, and someone who has led a cloistered life might seem naïve, trusting or ingenuous in speech.

milieu

Some of the best dialogue in contemporary fiction can be found in American crime novels. Conversational exchanges in an Elmore Leonard novel, for example, not only move the plot along and reveal aspects of personality, they also convey the milieu—that is, the strata of belief systems and attitudes—of the characters and others like them.

power relationship

Dialogue reveals the power relationships that exist between people. The conversation between a teacher and a pupil, or parent and child, or colonel and corporal, will show a relationship of authority and obedience (or authority and resistance). Note too, that people vary the register and tone of their speech according to the situations they find themselves in; for example, a doctor might speak sophisticatedly with her colleagues, simply with a child patient and nervously with her overbearing mother.

other functions

The spoken word is also used to inform, manipulate, negotiate, reinforce and mediate, or for self-protection, small talk and filling in awkward gaps. It gives pleasure, in the form of puns, jokes and recited poetry. It's ritualistic, as in the example of a husband asking his wife every evening, 'Did you have a good day?'

Many writers 'tag' characters, particularly minor characters, with a speech mannerism. The man who says repeatedly, 'I'm no expert, but…' or 'That's my girl' or 'See if I'm wrong', is both quickly identified in a scene and revealing an aspect of his personality.

Note also that not all dialogue is responsive. A character who responds tangentially or obliquely to a question or statement may be evasive or unable to come to terms with what has been said. For example:

'Have you been taking money from the till?' I demanded.

'There's been a lot of that going on lately,' he replied.

DRAMATISING SCENES

The next main use of dialogue is to render scenes—particularly important ones—more immediate, alive and forceful to the reader. Some scenes need not be dramatised, of course—a conversation about the weather or the price of petrol may be omitted, or merely reported, *unless* it's making necessary points about the characters and the patterns of their lives. Other scenes demand to be dramatised so that their impact is not lost. A declaration of hate or love, an insult, a reprimand or a job sacking are important and urgent in real life and should be so in fiction, too.

Note how flat and remote the following scene is when reported rather than dramatised:

> When Jean found Martin in her kitchen after his escape from the internment camp she explained that he should not try to see his children. She explained that they had been tormented by other children and it would only add to their unhappiness and confusion to find him there. Martin was indignant and accused Jean of wanting his children to forget him. Jean told him not to be silly. At that moment the two children, woken by the raised voices, entered the room. They didn't recognise Martin at first. When Jean took them back to bed Martin followed and, despite Jean's protests, kissed them goodnight. They seemed unresponsive and embarrassed to see him, and were relieved when he finally left the room.

This key scene is lost to the reader. There is no reason why readers should care about the characters or the outcome. But if it's dramatised there is a quickening of the pace, and it's more forceful and immediate:

'It hasn't been easy for them,' Jean said. 'Cruel comments at school, people staring at them in the street.'

'You've been very good to them, and to me,' Martin said.

Jean looked at him unhappily. 'The thing is, Martin, they don't know you've escaped. I haven't told them yet. I thought it would only confuse them.'

Martin frowned. 'They don't know?'

'No. So it's going to be very upsetting for them to find you here in the morning.'

'Upsetting to see their own father?'

'In the circumstances, yes. I think it would be best if you were to hide until they're at school. They need never know you've been here.'

'You want them to forget me,' Martin said.

'Don't be silly. I don't want them upset, that's all.'

'Before I know it,' Martin said, 'you will be sending them to their mother. You think an immoral waster is better for them.'

'Oh grow up, for goodness' sake.'

The door opened. Paul came in, rubbing his eyes, his pyjamas twisted this way and that. 'I can't sleep,' he said. Then he saw Martin and froze.

Nina appeared behind him, saying, 'You come back to bed at once. Sorry, Auntie Jean.'

Nina glanced at the visitor as though to express an apology, and saw who he was. Her face grew closed and absorbed. She had unbraided her hair. Threaded in the gathered wrists and collar of her nightdress were pale yellow ribbons.

'It's Dad,' Paul said, pointing suddenly. He looked at Nina. 'Dad's home.'

Jean clapped her hands. 'Off to bed, both of you. It's late.'

The matter was out of Martin's hands now. Their voices receded to another part of the house, and he was left with a likeness of them, an outline struck against the light that pours through an open door.

And so he followed them. At the door to the children's bedroom he said to Jean, 'I will kiss them goodnight.'

'*Martin!*'

'Just a kiss goodnight.'

The children's beds were separated by a brown carpet off-cut. The wardrobe was massive, its mirror spotty and silvered. In a club chair at the foot of Nina's bed sat a doll with a white, unlovely face. Paul owned a chart of military aircraft silhouettes. Not even an internee with barbed-wire disease was as impoverished as Martin's children.

They lay still and quiet as he leaned down to kiss them.

'Your old father is a bit dirty, isn't he? Such a journey I've had.'

Paul said, 'When are you going back to the gaol?'

Martin stiffened. 'I think tomorrow. Now that I have seen you again.'

The children sank deeper into their beds.

'But it is not a gaol. You must not listen when people tell you I am in a gaol.'

He hemmed and hawed on the carpet strip between their beds. 'Did you receive the pictures I made for you?' He looked around the room. 'You should have them on the walls. Didn't you like them?'

Nina made adjustments to her top sheet. Paul sat up and pointed at the wardrobe. 'We put some of them in there.'

Martin gathered himself. He told them it was late; it was time they were asleep. He said goodnight and switched off the light. Disburdened, they brightly cried, 'Goodnight.'

(Garry Disher, *The Stencil Man*)

The addition of action and dialogue has 'lifted' this passage. We learn a little more about the characters' personalities, too: Jean is sensible, patient, compassionate, while Martin is too ready to take offence and not think things through.

REVEALING PLOT INFORMATION

The third main use of dialogue is to provide plot or background information. For example, a short, skilfully handled dialogue scene can infer past events (thus saving on flashbacks), clarify the true nature of a relationship, or reveal what a character has been doing 'off-stage' during the main action.

Read the following passage, a telephone conversation that opens a story. What are you learning about the characters, their situation and matters prior to this scene?

'Sweetie pie, it's not too late, you know.'

'For God's sake, Dad,' the girl said, *'I'm all right!'*

'You don't want to come home?'

'No! For the hundredth time.'

'Your mother and I were saying last night how much you enjoyed Paris that time. Remember? I could have the tickets by lunchtime and you could be there tomorrow. Stay a few months, give yourself time to think things through. We both thought—'

'No thanks,' said the girl, stabbing the ashtray with her cigarette. 'Dad, I know you're busy—'

'What was wrong with Rick? Or Alan? Your mother and I thought they were both fine young—'

'Dad, I have to hang up now. I can hear Pete's bike.'

'Wonderful,' said the father. 'I suppose he still carts you around on the back of it like some moll?'

As you can see, a great deal of essential information has been packed into a short passage. We learn that a young woman from a well-to-do family has gone to live with a man who seems disreputable to her parents. The parents are wealthy and arrogant enough to interfere, even at this late stage, offering a bribe when emotional appeals fail. We can imagine the arguments and recriminations that must have ensued when the young woman had first announced that she was leaving the family home. The father keeps citing the mother's words in order to bolster his argument but the daughter has heard it all before and attempts to end the conversation. There is also a hint that she doesn't want her boyfriend to catch her talking to her parents, and you might ask yourselves why.

Note too, how quickly and naturally information has been conveyed. The dialogue doesn't explain, lecture or sound unnatural, as in the following passage:

'Sweetie pie, if you are having second thoughts about leaving home to live with the bikie, Pete, then I'm happy to pay for you to go overseas to think things through.'

'No thanks,' said the girl, 'we went through this before I left home and I don't want you using your vast wealth to pay me off.'

SOME DOS AND DON'TS

function

Choose what information is best provided by dialogue and what is best given through narration, bearing in mind that where there is dialogue there is a scene, and so flashbacks and passages of exposition will interrupt the flow. As you re-read your novels and stories, ask yourself what the purpose of each conversational exchange is, deleting those that serve no useful function and tightening those that threaten short-story economy.

Since the function of dialogue is to develop aspects of a character, dramatise scenes or provide information to the reader (and to other characters), non-functional dialogue like 'Please pass the butter' may be wasted or intrusive, even though people in real life say these sorts of things. Always ask how essential a passage of dialogue is. If 'Please pass the butter' provides a little domestic touch at just the right moment, reminds the reader where the action is taking place, relieves tension in an argument, or characterises a homely person or atmosphere, then clearly it isn't wasted or intrusive.

quirks of speech

Dialogue in a story or novel is never as random or tangential as it is in real life, where people ramble, use incomplete sentences, stutter, mis-pronounce words and punctuate their utterances with 'um' and 'er'. It's best simply to suggest, or say outright, that Michael stutters, Dominique is French or Ellen's sentences trail away.

At the same time, remember that the habits, mannerisms and difficulties of speech may do more than simply 'tag' characters and help readers differentiate between them. It could be that Michael's stutter has long-term ramifications for him and the action of the story.

he said; she said

Many beginner writers believe that the word 'said' is boring, especially if it's repeated, and so over-use variations like *exclaimed*, *intoned*, *declared* and *queried*. There is nothing wrong with 'said'. It does the job well and is short and unobtrusive. Often the context helps the reader hear the voice; for example, 'inquired' and 'exclaimed' are redundant in the following sentences:

'How are you getting on?' he inquired.

When England won the World Cup, Jim and his mates hugged one another, danced madly around the room and exclaimed, 'We've won, we've won!'

indirect speech

Internal dialogue can be used to good effect. In the following passage, indirect speech conveys a sense of distinctive voices speaking aloud:

Tom said that he wanted her to come to the football. He was getting sick and tired of the way she always made excuses not to go. But she hated football. Why should she have to go to the stupid football just because they were going out together? After all, she didn't expect him to go to her office parties, did she? He was getting too possessive and she was sick of it.

Thoughts may also be written in the form of indirect speech:

Some deal, he thought. My mates will kill me if I grass on them, the cops will gaol me if I don't.

Or be conveyed in a less immediate way:

He thought that it wasn't much of a deal to be asked to choose between informing on his mates and being sent to gaol.

Note that because thoughts are not uttered aloud it's not necessary to use quotation marks, and because they're internal and private it's not necessary to conclude them with 'he thought to himself'.

LISTEN

Many new writers avoid using dialogue for fear of their characters sounding stilted and unnatural. Try to develop an ear for dialogue by listening to people from all walks of life and making note of what makes their words and expressions distinctive. Note also the context in which you heard them, hidden meanings, and the personalities of the speakers, and as you write a passage of dialogue read it aloud to see if it rings true.

six

POINT OF VIEW

I am dead against art's being self-expression. I see an inherent failure in any story which fails to detach itself from the author.
ELIZABETH BOWEN

The voice and perspective of the narrator gives a story or novel its *point of view*. This determines the way readers gain their information, and governs the view they have on events, characters and themes. The expressions 'first-', 'second-' and 'third-person' do not mean that there are one, two or three characters present but are simply grammatical terms describing the use of 'I', 'you' or 'he/she'. For example, the sentence 'I thought my heart would break when she left me' is written in the first-person point of view; 'You thought your heart would break when she left you' is written in the second-person point of view; and 'Fred thought his heart would break when she left him' is written in the third-person point of view.

DETERMINING THE POINT OF VIEW

It's important to find the right voice for a work of fiction because it's the doorway through which the reader enters the story. Voice involves issues of tone, characterisation, viewpoint and the reader's relationship to the material.

The doubts, anxieties, frustrations and torn-up drafts that mark my experience of beginning a new story or novel owe almost everything to trying to get the voice right. Selecting an appropriate point of view is only part of the process. The American novelist E. L. Doctorow said that he'd spent years 'waiting for McIlvaine', the wry, shrewd, unimpressed newspaper editor who narrates his novel of 1870s New York, *The Waterworks*: 'You have to find the voice that allows you to write what you want to write. If you don't find the voice, you don't write the book.'

Often voice is not a problem. A certain voice may simply feel right, or seems the appropriate expression of the hero's personality, the writer's own voice, or the tone of the work. One kind of novel may require that a character is present in all of the scenes, another that everything is known about all of the characters. Perhaps a sophisticated adult's perception might be needed, or a naïve character's perceptions that are at odds with what the reader learns. For example, the first-person point of view best conveys the cheerful, wise-cracking, rough-diamond nature of a private eye; the limited third-person conveys a more distant atmosphere; omniscient (where the narrator knows all) and multiple viewpoints are effective in novels that depend for effect on the reader having a broad overview or knowing more than individual characters do.

The following sections discuss, in turn, how the third-, second- and first-person points of view work, and examine some of their variations and strengths and weaknesses. Each is illustrated by a brief scene taken from my (first-person) novel, *The Divine Wind*, rewritten accordingly. Note how altering the point of view can change the focus and tone of a work of fiction.

THIRD-PERSON POINT OF VIEW

Third-person is the most common point of view in fiction. The reader has a sense of a story being told *about* a character or set of characters rather than *by* a character (as in the first-person point of view).

Hart lived for Mitsy. When she bathed him, a kind of sad longing seemed to flow from her into him. It was as if she needed to heal, to negate death. She would smile at him, a distant, abstracted smile. She was the opposite of the bossy nurses.

As the days mounted, however, and no news came of her father, she grew more and more withdrawn. She seemed to accept that Zeke would never be found alive. She was clearly grieving, but the configuration of it was private, and Hart longed for her to talk to him.

An opportunity came one morning after she'd been away for three days. Hart had been a little frantic as a result, the shameful side of him saying that she'd had no right to abandon him, the generous side saying that of course she needed time alone to grieve, and to care for Sadako. And so when she walked in he burst out, 'I've missed you.'

Mitsy looked past him and fussed with the sheet at the foot of his bed. 'My mother needed me.'

Hart was about to say, 'I needed you too,' the response of a man who's upset and selfish and not thinking straight, but he stopped himself in time.

'How is she?'

Mitsy was not looking at him. Her mind seemed to be very far away. Suddenly she said, 'No-one understands. We need the body.'

He reached out and she let him close his hand over hers. It felt hot and alive but as tight as a rock. He knew, from his father's years of pearling, how important it was to the Japanese divers to bring a corpse back for burial.

'Is there some kind of prayer?' he asked. 'Some kind of ceremony to save him?'

'Oh, Hart.'

Mitsy knuckled both of her eyes and stood up. Hart sensed that he'd said something right this time, that he'd struck the right note, to acknowledge the *Japanese* side of Mitsy's nature.

limited third-person

The above example is limited third-person, for we don't stray from Hart's viewpoint. Although not as intimate as the first-person viewpoint, in which the narrator expresses thoughts and feelings directly to the reader, it can still carry an emotional load, encouraged by its detached perspective. It also offers opportunities for creating suspense if the reader remains in the dark along with the main character and—as in the first-person—it's possible to create a credibility gap between what the reader knows is the 'truth' and what the main character thinks is the truth. The strengths and subtleties of the limited third-person point of view are evident in J. M. Coetzee's Booker Prize-winning novel, *Disgrace*. We readers respond to the dark ironies and allegories present in the story and share the anxieties of the main character, even as we grow to realise, with him, that he often misreads situations or that his perspective on them lacks flexibility.

There can be disadvantages in using the limited third-person. For example, readers can't see all of the action that may be important to the story, although good writing can compensate. It's also less involving than the first-person point of view—which may be a good thing when the material is powerful and intense. In general, the writer should take into account the fact that readers can only go as far into the story as the main character goes, and that background or 'meanwhile, back at the ranch' material will have to be revealed in dialogue or other means.

omniscient third-person

Omniscient means 'all-knowing'. The narrator knows how all of the characters act, feel and think, knows the whole past and future of the events being described, and may refer to matters that have no direct relevance to the characters, such as changes to a district or town over hundreds of years. Omniscience can operate within one page (as an exercise try rewriting the above scene by going into Mitsy's mind as well as Hart's), or individual chapters or sections can be devoted to each character. Because we enter the minds of more than one character, it's possible to show what might be happening behind a main character's back. I use this device in the Wyatt crime novels to create tension, the intention being that the reader, privy to information that Wyatt doesn't gain until it's too late, is made more anxious about the outcome on his behalf.

In some omniscient novels there may also be a sense of the author's presence; for example, revealed in a bitter or ironic tone. Some nineteenth-century novelists liked to interrupt the narrative to instruct or make a point.

The third-person omniscient point of view works well in mass-market popular fiction in which readers are swept along by the action and are not required to speculate or infer anything. It was also commonly used in nineteenth-century novels, for example, those of Charles Dickens. Although the fiction of more recent times has probably tended to favour more limited viewpoints, the omniscient third-person is still very popular, especially in novels that deal with large casts, issues and sweeps of time.

There are certain disadvantages in using the omniscient third-person point of view. It's generally unsuitable for short stories, which owe a great deal of their effect to a concentrated focus. Readers tend to empathise with one or two main characters and may resent dividing their loyalties among several equally well-known characters. Suspense and tension can be weakened if everything is known, and readers might resent the intrusions, judgements or versatility of a 'know-all' narrator.

objective third-person

In the rarely used objective third-person no character's mind is entered—readers deduce the feelings and thoughts of the characters from what they say and do. It's rather like watching a film. The effect can be chilling and unremitting, as in the Ernest Hemingway short story, 'The Killers', but there are obvious drawbacks. It's harder to indicate complex feelings or a wide range of feelings—obvious feelings like anger are easier to depict. Since readers are unlikely to identify with characters they know little about, the external information (actions and dialogue) must be telling and subtle if it's to indicate an inner life adequately. A work that overcomes these shortcomings is the novel, *Vox*, by Nicholson Baker, in which a man and a woman—strangers—have a sexual encounter by telephone. Owing to the buoyant, tender and intimate nature of their conversation we learn a great deal about them.

SECOND-PERSON POINT OF VIEW

This rarely-used narrative voice seems to invite readers to imagine that they are someone else, or somewhere else, or what it would be like in a particular situation.

> It was Mitsy you lived for. When she bathed you, a kind of sad longing seemed to flow from her into you. It was as if she needed to heal, to negate death. She would smile at you, a distant, abstracted smile. She was the opposite of the bossy nurses.
>
> As the days mounted, however, and no news came of her father, she grew more and more withdrawn. She seemed to accept that Zeke would never be found alive. She was clearly grieving, but the configuration of it was private, and you longed for her to talk to you.
>
> An opportunity came one morning after she'd been away for three days. You'd been a little frantic as a result. Your shameful side said that she had no right to abandon you; your generous side said that of course she needed time alone to grieve, and care for Sadako.

When she walked in you burst out, 'I've missed you.'

Mitsy looked past you and fussed with the sheet at the foot of your bed. 'My mother needed me.'

You were about to say, 'I needed you too,' the kind of response people make when they're upset and selfish and not thinking straight, but you stopped yourself in time.

'How is she?'

Mitsy was not looking at you. Her mind was far away. Suddenly she said, 'No-one understands. We need the body.'

You reached out and she let you close your hand over hers. It felt hot and alive but as tight as a rock. You knew, from your father's years of pearling, how important it was to the Japanese divers to bring a corpse back for burial.

'Is there some kind of prayer?' you asked. 'Some kind of ceremony to save him?'

'Oh, Hart.'

Mitsy knuckled both of her eyes and stood up. You sensed that you'd said something right this time, that you'd struck the right note, to acknowledge the *Japanese* side of Mitsy's nature.

Second-person may also be the first-person in disguise, as in the following example:

'It's not easy being a writer. You go to your desk every day at nine o'clock, then spend the morning drinking endless cups of coffee, waiting for the ideas to flow. Your bank balance is in a parlous state and you wonder if this "how to write" book is going to make your fortune.'

That is, the reader is being asked to share an experience.

Very few novels or stories have been written exclusively in the second-person. It's most likely to be found in the form of a brief slide from the first- and third-person points of view for a particular effect, as in the opening paragraph of Chekhov's story, 'The Lament', where readers are asked to sympathise with a horse standing in the snow. Any extensive use of the second-person point of view means the repetition of 'you' and 'your', which can become irritating, but readers might like to examine *The Treatment*, a novel by the Australian writer Peter Kocan, and the short stories in Frederick Barthelme's *Moon Deluxe*.

Often the second-person has an uncomfortable edge, as though the characters are dissociating themselves from their morbid obsessions while simultaneously documenting them. Here is an example from my short story, 'Airship', about a man intent on getting revenge for all of the times he'd been kept awake by swimming-pool parties at the townhouse complex next door:

You took the valium with a scotch boost at eleven, but now it's two in the morning and you have heard every taxi, car and cry in the night. Guests come and go in the starlight on the sundeck. The sound system is apparently inside the pool-room, for you can't hear the music, only bass notes that reach you like repeated explosions underground.

Liz comes home at three. She prowls about in her Volkswagen, searching for a space. When you realise that she's begun a set of parking manoeuvres outside your window, you snap out the light. You continue to hold *Paris Trout* open, as though reading it in the dark. You'd begun it at half-past one. Its air of dread has leaked into the room.

Liz locks her car. 'You awake in there?' she whispers, close to the window box.

You lie still, waiting for the double click of her front door shutting, then put down the book. You stretch out on your back, your head on the pillow. Paris Trout believed that he would be shot in the back from below, so he'd clamped a lead plate to his bed base. Over at the Flamingo Gate they are winding down at last, for you can't hear the bass percussions any more. Cars start. People call good night, and one of them cries 'Born in the USA'. It is like a caste mark, a password, a trace of the night.

At four you peer through the curtain. They have switched off the sundeck spotlights.

You dress in black: jeans, T-shirt and Chinese slippers. You push your thumb against the pouring flap on the box of laundry powder and when that doesn't work you cut the perforations with a knife. You shake the spray can of paint. It rattles like a defective clock.

You partly open the front door. A distant siren, a cat in the alley, the police helicopter probing the laneways of Fitzroy with a searchlight. You open the door fully, step out, close it gently behind you. The day's heat is still locked into the brick wall.

And Liz says from her front step, 'Well, well, it's Indiana Jones.'

FIRST-PERSON POINT OF VIEW

In first-person stories and novels the narrator is actually a character in the story, either the main character or a relatively minor character observing the actions of others. Remember that this character is *fictional*: we are usually not listening to the author talking.

It was Mitsy I lived for. When she bathed me, a kind of sad longing seemed to flow from her into me. It was as if she needed to heal, to negate death. She would smile at me, a distant, abstracted smile. She was the opposite of the bossy nurses.

As the days mounted, however, and no news came of her father, she grew more and more withdrawn. She seemed to accept that Zeke would never be found alive. She was clearly grieving, but the configuration of it was private and I longed for her to talk to me.

An opportunity came one morning after she'd been away for three days. I was a little frantic by then. The shameful side of me said that she had no right to abandon me; the generous side said that of course she needed time alone to grieve, and to care for Sadako.

When she walked in I burst out, 'I've missed you.'

Mitsy looked past me and fussed with the sheet at the foot of the bed. 'My mother needed me.'

I was about to say, 'I needed you too,' the kind of response you make when you're upset and selfish and not thinking straight, but I stopped myself in time.

'How is she?'

Mitsy was not looking at me. Her mind was far away. Suddenly she said, 'No-one understands. We need the body.'

I reached out and she let me close my hand over hers. It felt hot and alive but as tight as a rock. I knew, from my father's years of pearling, how important it was to the Japanese divers to bring a corpse back for burial.

'Is there some kind of prayer?' I asked. 'Some kind of ceremony to save him?'

'Oh, Hart.'

She knuckled both of her eyes and stood up. I sensed that I'd said something right this time, that I'd struck the right note, to acknowledge the *Japanese* side of her nature.

The first-person can be a very effective device, for it allows readers intimate access to the doubts, hopes, fears and machinations of the narrator, and is particularly immediate if combined with the present tense, as in the case of Tillie Olsen's short story, 'I Stand Here Ironing' and many of the stories of the American 'dirty realists', Raymond Carver and Bobbie Ann Mason. Here is an example from my novel, *The Apostle Bird*:

I look up from watering the sweetcorn plants. Kitty has appeared at the edge of the lawn, wearing a loose white cotton dress, sockless tennis shoes and a straw cowboy hat. She looks unbothered by her long walk through the heat, and at once I feel too hot, too grimy, too awkward to be near her.

Before I can avoid it she is crouching next to me, saying, 'Perhaps we could build a shallow depression at the base of each plant to hold the water.'

After a while I begin to relax. Kitty and I work well together, Kitty using her hands as trowels to shape the dirt, me fetching and pouring the water. I can't pour too quickly, for the soil is slow to absorb the water, and so I'm often squatting next to Kitty for some time in ticking silence, watching the water pool then soak away in her little dams. From time to time she scoops the soil, halting a water break.

I can scarcely breathe for being so close to her. She has bunched her dress around her thighs. Her bare legs are dusty now, here and there streaked with a water splash or perspiration. I can smell the wet earth and I can smell Kitty, a hint of salt, of sunheated cotton and skin. Her breasts shift beneath her dress. I try to swallow. Whenever she moves on her haunches to ease the strain in her legs, she brushes against me. I'm sure she's unaware of it. I don't know what to do. I can't name my feelings but they are very strong. She's not once looked at Humphrey sprawled on the verandah. I'm hard, in agony, and forced to turn away.

First-person stories and novels sometimes create a credibility gap between what the reader knows and what the narrator knows. The narrator of Molly Keane's *Good Behaviour* is not aware of her brother's homosexual relationship with another man, and the narrator of Iris Murdoch's *The Sea, The Sea* deceives himself—and, for a time, the reader too—that he can rescue his old flame from an apparently unhappy marriage. Having to rely on an unreliable witness creates an interesting tension. This unreliability may be due to such factors as the main character's lies, self-deceit, mistaken perceptions, vanity or incompetence, or lack of intelligence, insight, experience or wisdom. It's a difficult device for the writer, however, for it depends on the reader second-guessing and seeing through the narrator, independently grasping the truth about a situation which the narrator is blind to.

There are several forms in which the first-person point of view may be used (and two or more may co-exist in a story or novel).

subjective narration

Almost all first-person stories and novels are subjective, which means that the narrator is moved by his or her own thoughts, emotions and attitudes, as in the above example from *The Apostle Bird*.

objective narration

This is the opposite of subjective narration in that the narrator reports external realities (descriptions, what is said and done) *only*, not his or her inner life of thoughts, emotions and attitudes (although these may be revealed aloud in dialogue). It's like watching a film: readers are obliged to infer information from tone of voice, for example, or from a punch or a kiss. Most writers use the objective first-person only occasionally, to create extra tension or resonance, but Rudolph Wurlitzer's novel, *Quake*, is an example of a complete work written in this point of view. The action of the novel spans a severe earthquake and its aftermath of urban chaos and anarchy. The narrator is witness to, and victim of, many terrible things, but his account of them is eerily flat and unemotional—which renders them all the more powerful to the reader.

observer narration

The classic example already noted is F. Scott Fitzgerald's novel, *The Great Gatsby*, in which a 'minor' character, Nick Carraway, observes the doomed relationship between major characters Gatsby and Daisy. Carraway may appear to be a minor character, but note that he's the only one to change and reflect at the end of the novel.

detached autobiography

In this form of narration, some time has passed since the events being narrated occurred, and the narrator is looking back with a new understanding, a clearer, wiser, more mature outlook than the one held at the time. See *Rebecca* by Daphne du Maurier, and several of the stories in Richard Ford's collection, *Rock Springs*. Ford acknowledges a debt to the American writer, Sherwood Anderson, in some of whose stories

> an adult narrator tells a series of events recalled from his childhood, a seemingly simpler time, when the speaker was but a receptor—though a keen one—for whom life's memorable moments became the stuff of later inquiry and recognition.

multiple viewpoints

When several characters give separate first-person accounts of their part in the story, we see it from multiple and different points of view. A writer's skill is tested here because several distinct and individual personalities must be created, each with its own voice. An interesting tension can develop when the characters' interpretations of an event do not agree. Whom should the reader trust or believe? Each character's account will be influenced by personality, prejudice, closeness to the events and limitations to understanding. When police interview the witnesses to an accident or crime, for instance, no two accounts are exactly alike.

In terms of structure, multiple viewpoints can work in different ways. After the action has taken place each character gives his or her version of what happened, or, more commonly, as the events unfold the narrative might move from one character to another and back again, according to the degree of their involvement, until the final scenes, thereby creating suspense about the outcome, as in Barbara Kingsolver's novel, *The Poisonwood Bible*. Multiple viewpoints is best suited to the novel, as in Wilkie Collins's *The Woman in White*, Graham Swift's *Last Orders* or Amy Tan's *The Joy Luck Club*; if used in short stories it should not involve too many characters, as there is not usually the space to develop each point of view effectively.

interior monologue

In a monologue only one person is speaking. In an interior monologue we 'hear' the narrator's thoughts; nothing is uttered aloud. Its equivalent in the theatre is the soliloquy. There are two main types of monologue: a narrator caught in the present, and a narrator reflecting on past events as they impinge on the present. Given that a narrator's identity, personality and circumstances should be unique, the *way* the story is told is as important as *what* is told.

One of the best-known examples is 'I Stand Here Ironing', by the American short-story writer Tillie Olsen. Nothing happens in Olsen's story; a woman is ironing a dress, that's all. The action is internal, the narrator reassessing a difficult relationship as a result of a telephone call. At the end she comes to understand that she'd done the best she could, given the circumstances—but this simple insight, and her journey toward it, are quietly devastating.

Olsen's story is structured as a frame-within-a-frame. A first-person, present-tense outer frame introduces the narrator at her moment of crisis; flashbacks accounting for it comprise the inner frame.

There are certain limitations to the interior monologue. Although attempted in novels such as Elliot Perlman's *Three Dollars*, it's difficult to sustain in a long work and is more convincing when used with other techniques, or alternated between several characters, as in Virginia Woolf's *The Waves*, for otherwise we find ourselves wondering at a narrator's ability to address him- or herself for several hundred pages. Another limitation relates to tension and suspense. Strictly speaking, nothing happens in a story told through flashbacks. Since events are not experienced or anticipated in the here and now but recalled some time after they've happened, the reader and the narrator cannot be in doubt about the outcomes. We don't travel with the narrator, in other words. Not enough is at stake. Since we know that the narrator has survived, we're not encouraged to ask that vital question: *What's going to happen next?* This limitation is especially noticeable in a novel, although good writers may overcome it to some extent by dramatising key scenes, or achieve tension by setting a narrator in a strange situation and then backtracking to explain how he or she got to be in it.

dramatic monologue

In this rarely used form we again have one voice, but this time the narrator is talking aloud, as in one side of a telephone conversation, for example. If done skilfully, readers can learn, from the dialogue and implied tone, not only things about the narrator but also about the unheard respondent. In Ring Lardner's short story, 'Haircut', a barber talks without interruption to a customer. For examples in another medium, listen to the recordings of certain comedy sketches by Lily Tomlin, Barry Humphries and Bob Newhart.

letter narration

A story may be told in one letter only, or a series of letters by one person over time, or in an exchange of letters between two or more people. Some otherwise straightforward novels and stories incorporate letters or parts of letters. For examples of letter narration, see the Frank Moorhouse short story, 'Letters to Twiggy' and the Jean Webster novel, *Daddy Longlegs*.

diary narration

A story or novel told in the form of diary entries (for example, tracing a personal crisis or a relationship) shows reactions to events as they happen and also reveals states of mind. John Fowles's *The Collector* is told partly by diary entries. A sequential diary or journal offers opportunities of both immediate present experience and later reflection on that experience.

frame-within-a-frame

This is a rather old-fashioned but effective device. One of the best-known examples is Emily Brontë's novel, *Wuthering Heights*. The outer frame is represented by the voice of the character Lockwood, introduced at the start and followed through to the end. The inner frame, beginning at Chapter 4, is in the voice of the character Nelly, as she tells Lockwood about life at Wuthering Heights some time earlier, especially concerning the relationship between Cathy and Heathcliff. One problem for the writer is how active or passive the outer-frame narrator should be, and how often or to what degree he or she should comment on the inner story; but done well it can be suspenseful.

I was also reminded, when reading a manuscript in this form which had been entered for a competition, that the challenge for the writer lies in foregrounding the inner story to make it immediate and absorbing, for logically it has already happened and is being related second-hand, so why should readers care about the outcome? Also, if there are too many stories within a story the focus can become blurred and the tension frayed.

stream of consciousness

Some of the above forms might use the 'stream of consciousness' technique, by which the narrator's consciousness pours forth in a stream of apparently unrelated thoughts and feelings. The writer is usually imposing some sort of order on the material, and for a particular purpose, however. The stream of consciousness technique was used by some significant writers of the early part of the twentieth century, such as Virginia Woolf and James Joyce. It's sometimes used to demonstrate the mental disintegration of a character, or a character influenced by drugs or alcohol.

limitations of the first-person point of view

There are certain limitations to the first-person point of view. The reader can go only as far into the story as the narrator goes and can witness only scenes that the narrator witnesses. There are things that the narrator couldn't or shouldn't possibly know, although he or she may speculate or be told things.

On the other hand, first-person is the favoured point of view in private-eye novels because readers are just as much in the dark as the hero they have come to know, like and trust.

Sometimes it can be monotonous to listen to a voice that keeps saying 'I'. First-person characters, no matter how dull their lives or how tedious they might seem if we met them in real life, should at least be interesting to 'listen to' on the page. A voice that is boring, or too self-interested or self-conscious, might risk losing the reader's interest. And how are some sorts of information to be given? Characters shouldn't say or think things they already know, just for the sake of informing the reader. Exposition will sound forced and unnatural unless it's from a character analysing past events. If it's necessary to inform readers what characters look like, writers try to find fresh ways of doing so, like 'Fred told me he liked the blonde streaks in my hair' or 'The other librarians could reach books on the upper shelves with ease, but I had to use a ladder'.

In general, readers have to rely on the narrator for information, and it helps writers to be aware of all the factors limiting or colouring the narrator's perceptions, such as age, gender, cultural background, social class, level of education, value system and levels of experience and wisdom. Sometimes the monologue narrative form can puzzle or irritate readers when it's not clear who is talking or where or why they are talking.

The first-person present-tense combination is often used to good effect in novellas and short stories, but it too has certain limitations; for example, the narrator can't logically stop to reflect, assess or describe, particularly in times of action or stress, for the story is meant to be unfolding as we read:

He's on top of me now, punching, then squeezing my neck, his weight holding me down. But there is a kind of sadness and regret on his face, too, and I'm reminded of my old headmaster, a man who used the strap when necessary but always with that same expression of regret. The minutes pass. My consciousness begins to fade.

Another potential problem of the first-person is that it can give the impression of a narrator who is more literate, articulate, or perceptive than would seem likely, given his or her background or circumstances. I faced this issue when writing *The Bamboo Flute*, in which the narrator is a twelve-year-old boy. A certain degree of licence is allowable, I believe, and if the writing and the narrator are strong and convincing, then readers will suspend disbelief.

But there are instances when readers might not suspend *judging* the narrator. Most of us start reading a novel or story in the expectation of liking or at least being on the side of the main character, and most of the time that expectation is rewarded, but sometimes we encounter narrators who are not likeable or worth supporting. Is that our shortcoming or the writer's? Or is it a shortcoming at all? Readers who are not widely read in fiction, or are more comfortable with the less intimate third-person point of view, may recoil from narrators who are supercilious, self-righteous, affected or downright nasty. It could also be that the writer is at fault for failing to strike the right tone or unintentionally creating a whingeing voice and unappealing character traits. But are we always supposed to like or barrack for the narrator? Good writers can *intentionally* create unappealing narrators but still hold and absorb the reader. The narrator of John Banville's novel,

The Untouchable, is a spy, a traitor, a snob and a boozy, campy aesthete. He is alternately caustic, self-pitying, unreliable and detached—yet his voice is believable, engaging and ironic, and Banville's prose is exquisite, and so we read on.

SHIFTING AND COMBINING POINTS OF VIEW

Although fiction writers often try a different point of view at the drafting stage if the original proves unsuitable or if they're 'blocked', most tend not to combine a range of viewpoints in a story or novel. It can be an effective device, however. The main character in Margaret Atwood's *The Edible Woman* is revealed through the first- and then the third-person points of view. The change occurs at the mid-point of the novel, at a key stage in the main character's life. So too, there is a constant shifting and merging of viewpoints in Keri Hulme's *The Bone People*. Kate Atkinson's novel, *Behind the Scenes at the Museum*, has a first-person outer frame, which enables the narrator to slip into the third-person for extended periods in order to tell the past stories of several of her forebears.

Point of view shifts are more likely to work in a novel than a short story. There should also be good technical or artistic reasons for it (for example, to give an alternative perspective). To avoid causing unnecessary confusion to readers, try indicating the change with an appropriate device, such as a new chapter or a line space in the text.

Finally, beware of the author's big mouth. Unless your work is deliberately postmodern in the sense of creating a story or novel and simultaneously commenting on the *process* of creating it, as John Fowles does in *The French Lieutenant's Woman*, try to avoid breaking in to explain or instruct. In general, trust your readers to get the point.

NARRATIVE DISTANCE

This is not a problem or an issue but an observation I wish to make. There has been a shift, it seems to me, from the sort of traditional novel practised by Henry James or Saul Bellow, in which readers see through the eyes of the characters to an intimate degree, to novels like Anne Tyler's *The Accidental Tourist*, which use meticulous, literal description and a long narrative distance, in which the author is quite detached, a viewer rather than an interpreter. Although sharply observed, characters seem flatter, and almost like caricatures.

seven

PLOT

> *I feel that art has something to do with the*
> *achievement of stillness in the midst of chaos.*
> SAUL BELLOW

'I loved his first book.'

'What's it about?'

'It's about a man, dying of cancer, who visits all of his old lovers one after the other to say goodbye...'

I don't know if there's ever been a short story or novel with the above plot, but you've no doubt had many conversations like this one. Plots may be simple, intricate or apparently non-existent, and certain plot situations (for example, a character torn between two lovers) appear again and again in literature, yet plot continues to be one of our basic measures of a short story or a novel.

SOME DEFINITIONS

Plot is more than simply *what happens* in a work of fiction. It may be understood in a variety of ways.

Plot is what happens in a story or novel, and *why* it happens—in other words, plot is causality at work (however well hidden). As E. M. Forster explained, '"The king died and then the queen died" is a story. "The king died and then the queen died of grief" is a plot.' There is little appeal in a story or novel of the kind: A happened and then B happened and then C happened...

Plot is the arrangement of scenes and actions to convey a theme.

Plot is not life; plot is an author's manoeuvring of events to make a point.

Plot is what characters do; actions and motives spring from characters and react upon them.

Plot grows out of conflict. It is a series of actions that explore a character's efforts to deal with conflict.

Plot provides momentum, with storyline and character development working hand in hand to engage the reader's emotional interest until a novel, say, is better on page 250 than it is on page 25.

PLOT AND CHARACTER

Graham Greene once said: 'The novel is an unknown man and I have to find him', and most fiction writers would argue that their characters shape their plots. But no matter what sort of initiating idea you may have for a story or novel—a character, a place, an image, a theme or abstract notion—character will ultimately determine the way you enter, tell and shape it. If personality and motivation are thoroughly understood then plotting becomes easier and characters will seem alive and believable on the page. As with real people, the lives of fictional characters are shaped according to their personalities and experiences, the lessons they've learned or failed to learn, and their responses to change and stress. Plots emerge as fictional characters search for a way out of difficulties, their struggles generating conflict and tension within themselves and with other characters. They may encounter interference, act irrationally, fail to act, or find alternative solutions, but reader interest is maintained by the implied question: Will he or she succeed?

Of course, many writers write without thinking of plot. Michael Ondaatje has described his method as 'an avoidance of plot'. Rather, he works by assembling layers of voices, memory fragments and shifting viewpoints, actions and time frames. Even so, there is ultimately a sense of a story unfolding in his novels.

As your plots take shape with your characters, be wary of imposing plot on the characters or indulging in character at the expense of a good plot. Try to juggle the two elements, drawing in and holding the reader with the storyline while also testing the characters' actions and decisions with these sorts of questions: Would he do that, given the sort of person he is? What does she want at this point? Where did he learn to do those things? What would result if she did this instead of that?

It should be apparent by now that this chapter is best read in conjunction with the chapters on Ideas for Stories and Novels, Planning and Structure.

As an exercise, identify a crucial turning point for the main character of one of your stories or novels and rework it as though he or she had decided upon a different course of action.

PLOT AND CONFLICT

It can be helpful to think of plot in terms of conflict, in which characters wrestle with doubts, problems or challenging situations. In most traditional stories and novels, conflict will be one of two kinds: trying against opposition to achieve a goal, or having to choose between two courses of action or values of equal strength. In the case of characters forced to choose, the dilemma is more intense if the choices available are equally undesirable.

There are many types of conflict. Even if the source of conflict is external—a big-game hunter tracking a dangerous wounded lion, a worker called a 'scab' for refusing to join a strike, an employee competing with her friend for a job promotion—inner conflicts will grow out of them. These are the moral or ethical issues that characters face. Consider the 'scab' worker above: he may feel guilty for betraying his mates. There might be an added complication, or secondary conflict: for example, the worker's father, who has always been scornful of his son's abilities, is a past hero of the union: can the son bear to give his father further ammunition against him? These sorts of conflicting desires and pressures can, in fiction as in real life, give rise to powerful feelings and push characters into further action, which will advance or add twists to the plot.

conflict and reader interest

Conflict will be convincing to readers if they can see that it's significant to the characters, and that its outcome is of obvious importance to them—especially when difficult decisions are involved, with the good and bad of one course of action equal to the good and bad of the other. In fact, Jean-Paul Sartre claimed that the only decision that fictional characters should make is the one which will be regretted whichever way it's made. Always, the conflict should be plausible, the reader able to recognise what such a dilemma would be like for the characters, even in otherwise 'unrealistic' fiction such as science fiction and fantasy.

the role of conflict

The following questions might help you to determine the nature and purpose of conflict in stories and novels:

Who is the main character? That is, on whom will the action of the story have the greatest effect?

What is the focus of the conflict—internal, external, or both?

How is the conflict resolved? (For example, the main character succeeds, fails, succeeds but realises that the goal was wrong, learns to live with the conflict unresolved.)

'PLOTLESS' FICTION

From time to time you will encounter stories and novels in which the plots are non-existent, arbitrary or illogical. It may simply be that they're badly written, but writing, like all art forms, is open to innovation. The American novelist John Hawkes once stated: 'I began to write fiction on the assumption that the true enemies of the novel were plot, character, setting and theme.' Chapters 9 and 11 discuss some writers' rejection of plot in greater detail.

eight

PLANNING

My work habits are simple: long periods of thinking,
short periods of writing.
ERNEST HEMINGWAY

Some fiction writers say blithely that they never plan. Many plan a little, or occasionally, and a few plan in meticulous detail. Others write copious notes, find these turning into a story or novel, and then pause to plan it.

Should you plan? When should you plan? How should you plan? How detailed should a plan be, and how rigorously should you apply it?

TO PLAN OR NOT TO PLAN

Could it be that beginner writers need to plan and experienced writers don't? Let's look at the working methods of a range of contemporary novelists:

John Grisham always starts with a plot idea, not a character, and then writes 45-page outlines, with two paragraphs per chapter explaining what will happen next. P. D. James takes three years to write each of her novels, which includes eighteen months of plotting and planning before she starts to write. James Ellroy plans his novels thoroughly first. He wrote a 164-page outline of *White Jazz*, for example, and a 211-page outline of *L.A. Confidential*, admitting to a 15 per cent 'improvisation factor' in the 'fever-driven voice' of the final drafts. Sue Grafton works her mystery novels out on three levels: the *apparent* mystery, as understood by her detective and her readers, the *real* mystery, revealed at the end, and the turning point, revelation or peeling away that links the other two levels. An organised mind, and knowing exactly what she wants to say before she begins to write, allows Colleen McCullough to write a first draft quickly and cleanly, with no editing or correcting. John Irving also knows as much of the story as possible, if not the whole story, before he begins. Patience and planning add up to foreknowledge, he says, which gives authority to the voice and confidence in the telling. He claims that without knowing the story that lies ahead a writer would need to be *very* confident in the powers of the voice that told it.

In contrast, the American crime writer, Tony Hillerman, never knows exactly where the plot is headed when he begins a book. By the end of it he may have uncovered what the crime was, and what motivated it, but still not have worked out how to end the story. David Malouf often has no idea what's going to happen in the middle when he shapes a novel but does know what the ending will be. James Lee Burke doesn't allow himself to see more than two scenes around the corner, and he revises endlessly. Elmore Leonard doesn't plan but follows his instincts. He usually starts with an interesting character but isn't afraid to shine the spotlight on another character if the first one lacks interest or potential. David Foster explains his approach in this way:

> I've no idea where my stories are going. I've only the vaguest idea of what I'm doing, too, until it's done...I rely on intuition. Although...I work with words, ideas, characters and narratives, I do write a novel holistically. I don't start at the beginning and finish at the end. I work like a painter on a painting. I am still working on the first page as I am working on the last page...When a novel has reached publishable length I am on the alert for an ending.

If my own experience is any guide, I find that I need to plan my crime novels in meticulous detail in order to stay a step ahead of the reader, and avoid coincidences, dead ends, contradictory time-lines and unlikely outcomes. However, for my other fiction I tend to use only brief sketch plans, so that the writing is a voyage of discovery, stemming from the conjunction of a character, a situation and a sense of promise.

No doubt personality traits are a factor in why some fiction writers plan and others don't. Even so I would argue that the *thinking* a writer does before and during the writing of a story or novel is a form of planning, and most good fiction is achieved in a mixture of writing, planning, rewriting, finer planning and further revision, so the question of whether to plan or not is moot. My advice is that it may be useful for new writers to try planning their work, but they should not be afraid to abandon a plan, or the habit of meticulous planning, if their instincts tell them to.

WHEN SHOULD YOU PLAN?

A certain amount of planning can help if you're a new writer, feeling uncertain about a new project, or starting a complex work, but there are other instances where it may be advisable.

Most novels require more thought than most short stories, for example. Several characters usually means several sub-plots to juggle, and not only should the characters behave consistently, from convincing motives, but their various relationships with one another should be understandable. All the strands of the plot, and how they are interrelated, should be accounted for at the end. Also, the movement of a novel depends upon peaks and troughs (tension and the release of tension), creating and maintaining suspense, turning points, and resolutions. Without a certain amount of planning it may not be easy to hold so many factors in your head, let alone hope that you'll be able to weave them together elegantly and neatly.

In the case of genre fiction, certain conventions may apply. Take romance fiction, for example. There are many different kinds, such as traditional, Gothic, modern, hospital, teenage, historical, and thriller. They are heavily plotted and fast-moving, with few characters and few secondary characters. Long passages of description and introspection are rare. Their plots may evolve from a situation like this: A young woman, doing good works (as a governess on an outback cattle station, for example), is attracted to a young man. Various factors keep them apart, such as his unhappy and unsuitable involvement with another, more sophisticated woman. Further complications may delay the path of true love; the young woman becomes involved with a man who turns out to be a bounder, for example. At the end of the novel, perhaps as a result of a dramatic incident, the young man realises that the young woman is the one for him after all, and they acknowledge their love for each other. Readers know there'll be a happy outcome, but the writer will aim to make it appear that this time there won't be, to maintain the tension that pulls the reader along.

Experienced romance writers may write their novels quickly, without planning, but new romance novelists are well advised to read widely in the genre and plan according to the conventions of it. Indeed, some romance publishers provide 'tip sheets' for new writers.

Finally, it's not unusual for fiction writers to stop in the course of a novel or story to rethink what they've written and write a plan to get themselves out of trouble. Others begin their stories or novels without knowing what the ending will be until the writing is well advanced, at which stage they may then stop to plan the final stages. And many will *re*-plan as new ideas occur to them during the writing. If necessary they will go back and unravel and restitch the work to accommodate the new material—but only if the seams don't show. It's better to save a pleasing but unworkable idea, character or incident for a new piece of fiction than let it spoil the one you are working on.

HOW TO PLAN

There are no right or wrong methods of planning. Agatha Christie liked to muse on plot and character for several weeks as she went about her day-to-day domestic affairs, and then, when the story had taken shape to her satisfaction, sit down and write it. Many writers jot notes, queries and skeleton outlines on scraps of paper, at the beginning and as the need arises, constantly revising and discarding as they go, or write plot summaries and storylines, simple declarative sentences along the lines of 'and then, and then…' Some writers use a card system, marking characters, scenes and incidents on separate cards and shuffling them around as plot solutions, complications and contradictions arise. Others use whiteboards or pin butchers' paper to the wall, listing characters and their motives, goals and obstacles, tracing intersections and influences, and locating characters in terms of time and place. The planning might also involve *character planning*, in which the broad stages of a character's personality or growth are plotted. These kinds of mapping and diagramming can enable writers to view everything at a glance, which is important when managing a large cast.

Whatever your preferred approach, it's important to spot coincidences, contradictions, implausibilities and wasted material before it's too late, and also identify where, when and how your characters intersect with one another. A *timeline* or calendar of events and characters can be useful. I once wrote a crime novel in which, logically, one character received a letter on a Sunday, another character must have been in two places at a crucial stage of the plot, and a third character cropped up again after a gap of two hundred pages. Fortunately my editor identified these mistakes before the book went to print, but next time it might be a reader, so don't assume that an editor will always spot your contradictions.

Coincidences and convenient twists of fate happen in real

life (for example, a lottery win by a family who were about to lose everything), but should be used sparingly and cautiously in fiction so that they don't spill over into convenience (to write yourself out of a corner or conveniently end a troublesome story, for example).

Good planning can also help with pace and structure. No one wants to read a novel in which the pace is unrelievedly hectic, for example, or the central mystery is revealed too early, or tension is allowed to dissipate, or the reversals are telegraphed too obviously. Remember the role that causality plays: try withholding and delaying tactics to increase suspense, get readers to exercise their minds about the *wrong* person or problem, and ask yourself what the reader might want to happen next, then subvert it. Yes, these may be the 'tricks' of a mystery writer, but they will make even the most 'literary' novel more gripping.

For further information about the main stages of stories and novels, see the Chapters 9, 11 and 12.

TESTING A PLAN

Pay attention to character as well as storyline when you plan, so that you don't force unlikely actions onto characters or indulge in character at the expense of action. When thinking about both the main storyline and whether or not to use particular scenes or incidents, how to use them, and what their outcomes should be, I tend to ask questions like these: What does she want? Would he do that, given the sort of person he is? Where did she learn to do that? Is he motivated strongly enough to act *out* of character? How far is she likely to go to achieve her aims? What does he want more than anything else? What would happen if she did this instead of that? What is stopping him from doing this?

TRUST YOUR INSTINCTS

Never be bound to a plan. If in the course of writing a story or novel your instincts tell you to follow a different character or course of action, then revise or abandon your original plan—after satisfying yourself that the new direction will work, of course. I'm suspicious of writers who say that their characters take over from them; the writer should always be in control, I believe. Your characters might *surprise* you, but that's less to do with airy notions of the creative flame and more to do with working subconsciously.

nine

STRUCTURE

Has a drinking song ever been written by a drunken man? It is wrong to think that feeling is everything. In the arts, feeling is nothing without form.
GUSTAVE FLAUBERT

By structure I mean the overall shape of a story or novel. In most fiction there is a shift of some kind, but there are many ways of structuring this shift, varying from the linear, in which the events happen in chronological order, to the frankly experimental. This chapter looks at a range of structures and the factors that influence them, and at the internal structures, or building blocks—such as chapters, scenes, links and flashbacks—that hold a work together. It should be read in conjunction with the chapters on Plot, Planning and Point of View.

TRADITIONAL STRUCTURES

Most stories and novels follow a simple linear structure: events occur in chronological order through a beginning, a middle and an ending. These three stages may be understood as: the set-up, which introduces the main character (or characters) and central issue; the complication or conflict stage, in which the characters try to resolve matters, usually unsuccessfully at first; and finally, the resolution.

This may sound overly neat, and not suggestive of the diffusion and randomness of real life, but a skilful writer can transcend its limitations. On a simple level, William Golding's novel, *Lord of the Flies*, is a three-act adventure story, but it's also a powerful allegory about civilised values under strain, and the ending, while climactic, is not a happy closure but the beginning of a darker story.

The question: Whom will Emma marry? lies at the heart of Jane Austen's *Emma*, and the novel progresses through various complications to the resolution of that question, but the novel is also structured to tease and delude the reader. For example, we think at first that Harriet is the central figure; then, when it's apparent that Emma is, we're misled into thinking that Frank Churchill rather than Knightly will be her future husband.

SOME VARIATIONS

There is a sense of movement in each of the following examples, but their structures vary enormously.

Evan Connell's novel, *Mrs Bridge*, traces a woman's life story but is structured as a series of titled and numbered fragments, some no more than a paragraph long, others several pages long. Each is vivid and suggestive—a scene, a piece of exposition—but taken together are cumulative and give a rich picture of the main character and her family.

Milan Kundera's *The Unbearable Lightness of Being* uses the viewpoints of three main characters, together with a narrator, their stories ranging back and forth over the same events, giving their own perspectives.

As a way of telling the story of a young Englishwoman's attempts to find out more about the life of her aunt in India between the wars, Ruth Prawer Jhabvala's *Heat and Dust* intertwines the stories of the two women, one set in the present, the other in the past.

Elizabeth Jane Howard's *The Long View* starts in the present, with a woman aged in her sixties, but rather than go forward it goes back and back in time until she's a teenager.

Doris Lessing's *The Grass is Singing* starts with the ending, a violent death, then goes back to trace the events that led up to it.

Virginia Woolf's *Mrs Dalloway* tells several parallel stories, each involving a separate character. Most have only the most tenuous link to one another, yet the sum effect is of a whole day and a whole way of life revealed.

Penelope Lively's *Moon Tiger* is told via several characters, their voices ranging from first- to third-person point of view and back again, together with many shifts in time and setting.

Gabriel Garcia Marquez's *Chronicle of a Death Foretold* seems to circle around the central issue, in the past and in the present, until it begins to emerge.

Don DeLillo's *Libra* progresses on four separate but interwoven planes and time scales, which gradually merge toward the end of the novel. The first is the story of Lee

Harvey Oswald from childhood to death. The second is the Kennedy assassination plotters over the course of one year. The third is a scholar or investigator who seems to be putting the story together afterwards. The fourth is the insertion of the fragmentary, floating voices of several minor characters, such as Oswald's mother. As these diverse characters, times and viewpoints intrude, the novel's perspective keeps shifting, as it does in DeLillo's more recent novel, *Underworld*, which spans half a century and is told through the interpenetrating storylines of about twenty characters, some of whom have minor roles in early sections only to reappear later, at a different age and in a different part of the world, as the main protagonist.

Of course, point of view is deeply implicated in structure. Amy Tan's novel, *The Joy Luck Club*, is told through eight characters, with shifts between past and present tense and shifts in time and location, from contemporary San Francisco to China in the recent past. It's somehow circular, and somehow spreads out in ripples, yet at the end it solves a problem posed at the beginning, so it's linear as well.

Sena Naslund was conscious of musical structures when she wrote *Ahab's Wife*, in particular the varying movements of a symphony.

As explained in Chapter 6, Emily Brontë's novel, *Wuthering Heights*, uses a story-within-a-story, or frame-within-a-frame, structure.

The action of Alex Garland's *The Tesseract*, which begins with an attempted shooting and a chase on foot through city streets, and ends with the gunmen cornering their quarry, involves several characters, including witnesses and innocent bystanders. Garland tells a series of parallel stories about these characters, showing how unconnected lives can be brought together by one incident.

Sometimes writers use a mixture of narrative devices. Ursula LeGuin's *The Left Hand of Darkness* incorporates documents with more traditional narrative streams, and changes viewpoints, tenses and time frames. In Tobias Wolff's *The Barracks Thief* there is an indeterminate narrator and several shifts in viewpoint. Michael Ondaatje's *The Collected Works of Billy the Kid* shifts between prose, poetry, fact and fiction.

David Malouf has said that he doesn't think of 'the forward drive' of his novels as having to do with plot but with letting 'opposite and contradictory notions, temperaments and ways of life co-exist inside the narrative' in a way that 'suggests something of the real complexity and contradictoriness of the world one's trying to deal with'.

INNOVATIVE FICTION

In recent decades there has been an increasing tendency toward experimentation in fiction writing in response to new ventures in other art forms and dissatisfaction with the limitations of the traditional realist form.

Of course, there was also experimentation before recent times. Laurence Sterne's novel, *The Life and Opinions of Tristram Shandy* (1760), is about the process of writing fiction, and it broke new ground in terms of ideas and format. Many short stories of the nineteenth and twentieth centuries that are regarded as classics do not follow the classic pattern.

Chekhov's 'The Lady with the Little Dog' doesn't have the kind of movement associated with traditional short stories. In fact, many of his stories don't follow a course of events but appear to be passing moments, as though the middle and end were missing. There are also many stories and novels that employ such a mixture of modes that there is no unified impression, while in others there is no moment of truth for the main character and no shift of perspective.

Since the Second World War, and influenced by a number of South American, North American and European writers, there has been a more consistent and self-conscious experimentation in fiction writing. This new fiction is many-sided. One side of it is an interest in the process of creativity, in how fiction is made, the telling of the story rather than the story itself. Another is its incorporation of other modes of expression such as photography and graphics, and experimentation with fonts and layout. Some innovative writers eschew formal expression, charging that it's artificial or conceals the true nature of existence. Others create illusions and then destroy them, or use black humour and absurd reasoning to make their points or shock complacent audiences. Many mix real history with elements of the mythical, the fantastic and the bizarre. Some of Jorge Luis Borges's stories challenge two features of traditionally plotted fiction: the linear structure and careful explication of actions and events. Time, for Borges, is not necessarily continuous and made up of sequential events, and life may be subject to randomness and chance. Alain Robbe-Grillet gives only the sense impressions of his characters. No motives, ideas or values control the characters or influence his readers' subjective involvement with the story.

Some innovative writers strive for freedom from the constraints of doctrines, literary conventions and assumptions about life and human nature. They use fantasy and irony, make reference to other texts and textual analysis, remind readers of the writer's controlling hand, and renounce content. They deny any obligation to decision or resolution in their 'plots', and make no suppositions about motivation and personality in their 'characters'. The American short-story writer Donald Barthelme said: 'Fragments are the only forms I trust.'

Others claim that traditional fiction, with its themes, neat plots and resolutions, fails to explain or tackle the special problems of the modern age, such as the nuclear threat, increasing violence and the breakdown of old certainties about life. Traditional fiction, it is argued, has faith in history and human perfectibility; innovative writers argue that the world is governed by chance, coincidence and chaos, and so their fiction may be devoid of values or themes, apparently inconsequential, and directionless. They write about characters who are free of history, with no origins or destinations, who don't learn, have insights, make decisions or resolve difficulties.

Innovative fiction has been called irrational, pointless, difficult and self-indulgent. It doesn't seem to meet our expectations of what plot, characterisation, theme and resolution should be. Questions aren't answered—or even asked. The implied pact or trust between reader and writer has been severed. But such criticisms often miss the point. It's always been a function of art to push at the boundaries of form and taste, challenge preconceived notions, invite alternative ways of perceiving, and jolt complacent audiences.

WHAT INFLUENCES STRUCTURE?

Theme, subject, character, point of view, starting points, endings, the need to release information in stages: all contribute to the decisions a writer makes regarding structure. Sometimes the material itself will suggest the appropriate structure. The traditional linear form is best suited to crime, romance, western and other types of genre fiction, for example.

At other times the structure might emerge as the writer makes certain decisions regarding pace, hidden causal factors and the generation of suspense. Turning points, delaying tactics, surprises, reversals and other deliberate teasing devices all influence the internal structure even as the overall effect is one of forward movement.

Character-based or portrait fiction is more likely than plot-based fiction to range back and forth over time as it explores moods, atmospheres and the associative nature of memory and feeling.

The narrative point of view is also important (see Chapter 6); in a novel told in the omniscient third-person, for example, we may know everything that's happening to everybody, and why, but in the case of a first-person novel we know only what the narrator knows.

Writers also experiment for the sake of it, for ideological reasons, or out of frustration with the traditional forms of telling a story. When I wrote *The Sunken Road* I knew that I wanted to tell the life story of Anna Tolley, the main character, but felt a great weariness at the thought of beginning with her birth, then dutifully tracing her adolescent and mature years, and finally ending with her death. Besides, I also wanted to explore time and memory: the impression that things repeat themselves throughout life, the paradoxical sense that the more things change the more they stay the same, and the associative nature of memory. The linear structure didn't lend itself to these things, and so I structured the novel as a series of biographies in miniature, each four- or five-page chapter taking Anna from childhood to old age but dealing with a different theme each time, such as 'Christmas', 'love' and 'regret'. As details accumulate and hidden secrets come to the surface toward the end of the novel, there is a sense of forward movement.

BUILDING BLOCKS

the beginning

The ideal opening sentence or paragraph of a story or novel will arouse reader interest. It must deliver what it promises, however, and not simply startle for the sake of it. Typical beginnings may consist of a conversation, an incident, a panoramic view of a setting, an arresting statement or an absorbing atmosphere.

Note how the following opening sentences and paragraphs give promise of what is to come:

> This is a story, I suppose, about a failure of intelligence: the Rawlings' marriage was grounded in intelligence. (Doris Lessing, 'To Room Nineteen')

> No one knew where the Newspaper of Claremont Street went in her spare time. (Elizabeth Jolley, 'Pear Tree Dance')

> There is a sandbank somewhere at the end of Earth where ocean stops and welkin stops and the winds of the world

come to rest. They are chancy beings, like their cousins the Fates, and prone to sudden inhuman boisterousness—which stands to reason; they have never claimed to be human. Indeed, they affect to despise us and almost anything to do with us. Someone got under their guard though, once. They became aunties. (Keri Hulme, 'Te Kaihau/The Windeater')

In the final weeks of 1941, when I was adrift in life and my sister was missing in a war zone, my father offered our home as sanctuary to a young Japanese woman named Mitsy Sennosuke, unaware that I was in love with her. This was in Broome, in the north-west, at the time of the invasion of Malaya, when Japanese bombs were falling like silver rain and old certainties were crumbling, when some who had been our friends were now treated as aliens, transfigured by enmity and fear. (Garry Disher, *The Divine Wind*)

It took me two or three weeks to write the opening paragraph of *The Divine Wind*. I was trying to match the mood and tone of the book that I was 'dreaming' in my head: a voice at once reflective, hopeful and regretful. I also wanted to locate the story in place and time, and introduce the main players and central theme. The whole novel is contained in that first paragraph, if you like.

The children's writer, Allan Ahlberg, says of openings:

It's like the way a piece of knitting is defined by the first row of stitches on your needle. It is the first three or four sentences that establish the feel and rhythm of a book. The assumption is that writing a story is about coherence, logic and planning. For me it is about the sense and the sound of the words. It is like finding the perfect pair of gloves to go with the coat.

The most effective beginnings, especially in short fiction, occur at a point well advanced in the story or opening scene, for example just before or in the midst of a moment of crisis or change. Modern readers may lose interest with slow build-ups and excessive backgrounding. The first chapter of a novel should introduce the main character and the main issue, and end at a minor peak that will compel readers to turn to chapter two. The novel that opens with a large cast of characters, issues and details risks losing readers. Similarly, short stories should establish the main character and issue early, preferably on the first page. Suspense and tension are maintained if readers' questions about the outcome are not answered until the end: don't give away too much too soon.

In the first chapter of my crime novel, *Kickback*, the professional criminal, Wyatt, is down on his luck and obliged to accept a burglary commission and work with an unreliable younger criminal, Sugarfoot. At the end of the chapter the job has gone terribly wrong—the 'hook' that gets readers to want to read on. I also planted a slow burning fuse: Sugarfoot himself. Full of grievances as a result of Wyatt's contemptuous treatment of him, Sugarfoot 'explodes' into action several chapters later in the book. This is an example of causality and foreshadowing. However well buried, causality is a governing principle in fiction.

the middle

In the long middle stages of typical stories and novels the main character attempts to resolve the issue set up in the beginning. He or she might make mistakes, or uncover some keys to a mystery, or fail to act until it's too late, or be caught between various courses of action. Each situation gives promise of further situations, and tension remains unresolved.

In crime fiction in particular, a series of situations of doubtful outcome are presented progressively, building tension as the ending draws closer. At the same time, there may be an ever-present air of menace or suppressed violence, which may occasionally erupt into action.

But there's no reason why all fiction writers can't learn something from the crime writer's bag of tricks. *Pacing* is a vital consideration. A novel or story with an unrelenting headlong pace runs the same risk of alienating readers as a sluggish one. It can be an effective device to vary scenes that are full of tension, action and drama with slower, more reflective ones.

Place your *surprises* carefully. A critical betrayal lies at the heart of my crime novel, *Kickback*: if revealed too soon, the remainder of the novel would have lacked tension; if revealed too late, it would have seemed tacked on. Consider anticipating what your readers want or expect at a certain point (action, a love scene, an explanation, a betrayal) and either satisfy them or subvert their expectations with the unexpected (though not with a cheap trick but something plausible and logical in terms of character motivation and storyline).

Try to employ *delaying tactics*. Suspense in fiction often lies in questions like: Will she fall in love with him after all? Who committed the murder? Who betrayed her? What happens next? Will he get away with it? Readers want to know, and your task is to make them want to know *badly*. Frustrate them a little: get them to exercise their minds about a wrong or tangential issue or character; withhold key information until later; pause to consider related but less important matters; use unexpected reversals, and partial or doubtful outcomes.

Time your *turning points* well. There is often one toward the end of the middle part of a story or novel. It may be the point at which the main character begins to understand what is going on, or to take charge with a greater degree of confidence. It may be triggered by a hidden fact revealed, a mistake on the part of another character, an obstacle overcome, a lesson learned, a trap activated. It should not appear too late, but there may also be less vital (but no less surprising) turning points at the very end, when, for example, the apparent solution is only part of the real solution.

the end

Character and conflict have been introduced and explored, and now a resolution is drawing near. What is the most likely answer to the questions or problems faced by your characters? He'll get the girl? She'll unmask the killer? He'll be reconciled with his father? She'll understand herself a little better? He'll get his revenge? She'll uncover the loot? Order will be restored? You might like to read John Fowles's novel, *The French Lieutenant's Woman*, which is both a story about passion and prejudice in nineteenth-century England, and a novel about the craft of novel writing, and consequently offers us two alternative endings.

Ideally the ending should not drag on too long, over-explain, or introduce new material (in fact, it's been said that stories and novels can be improved dramatically if the beginning and ending were lopped off). Nor should it be tacked on for want of a more logical one but be the obvious extension of all that has happened before it. It shouldn't be clichéd ('I woke up and realised it was all a dream'), coincidental (an elderly woman discovers that her next-door neighbour is in fact the twin sister from whom she'd been separated at birth—stranger things have happened in *real life*, but they rarely convince in fiction), or a convenient cheap trick (it's known from evidence at the murder scene that the killer has a wooden leg, but the reader isn't informed until the last page that the butler, who has been present throughout the story, has a wooden leg).

Try to see your endings as being in the hands of your characters. If you know them well then they can lead you to the appropriate solution, one in keeping with their motives and personalities. This might include an 'open' ending rather than perfect closure; for example one in which the main character continues to be irresolute.

Endings need not be overly dramatic or obvious, either. They may simply:

- clarify a situation
- reveal an aspect of personality
- solve a problem
- relax tension
- answer a mystery
- show a change in a character
- show a character failing to change
- bring to the surface something that is hidden
- bring simplicity, order and clarity.

Finally, endings are unsatisfactory if they close a story or novel with a 'bump'. The best endings, without introducing new material, will encourage readers to speculate upon the story beyond this point. Such an ending will suggest change in the main character's situation, or, if nothing changes, let readers see that life will go on as before. After all, in real life resolutions are never fully satisfactory, tidy or complete. David Malouf has said of endings:

> I always want it to be not an ending. I don't want the curtain to come down. I want there to be some kind of suspension at the end of the book so that the narrative world goes on existing and so that things are not resolved. As if you could think of a note that would just go on sounding forever.

layering

In addition to their beginnings, middles and endings, stories and novels are constructed of *layers*. For example, a private eye's ongoing doubts about his abilities, or anxieties about his wife's fidelity, might overlay every stage of his search for a kidnapped heiress. This kind of layering adds complexity to the story and the main character, and poses questions (for example, 'Will he leave his wife?') that encourage suspense.

chapters

Chapters are stages in the development of a novel. Their equivalent in the short story is the scene, but they may themselves consist of one or more scenes.

It can be helpful to view chapters in terms of their *function* (usually one main task, which advances the story in some way), *content* (what happens, what is said, who is involved, where it takes place), *tone* (for example, menacing, joyous, reflective) and *links* to chapters that precede and follow them.

First chapters tend to introduce the main character, the central issue, the time and the setting, and give a sense of the voice throughout the work. The following chapters then elaborate on what has been set up in the first chapter. If there are several major characters then it's best to introduce them gradually. I once named nineteen characters in the first thirty pages of a crime novel with a complex plot. My editor wailed: 'Do we need all of these characters? Do we need them *now*? Do they deserve equal weight with one another?' It was a good lesson for my future first chapters.

It's best to end a chapter on a high point, for example, heightened tension, then either further tighten the screws or partly or wholly relieve the tension in the next or a later chapter. It's a basic but effective device for generating suspense and encouraging readers to read on.

scenes

Scenes are another of the main building blocks of stories and novels. They often work as stories in miniature, with characters, actions, dialogue (including thoughts), a setting, an appropriate atmosphere (for example, an *exhilarating* car chase; a *distressing* argument) and may have a point of emphasis such as red wine from an overturned glass spreading across a white tablecloth during an argument between lovers. Information is *shown*, not *told* or explained, thus creating a sense of immediacy that engages the reader. *Show, don't tell*, is a basic 'rule' of fiction writing. If Bill feels threatened because his wife Anne is attending lectures at the university then don't tell us so but show it in a scene comprising speech and actions. Scenes also have a shape—a beginning, a middle and an ending—that may describe a gradual build-up of tension leading to a resolution. Like chapters, they are linked to scenes that precede and follow them.

When writing a scene it's useful to ask yourself: What is my purpose here? Does this scene advance the story or illustrate the theme, or is it an indulgence or an unnecessary repetition? Is the action significant enough to be a scene? Have I entered as late as possible—or too early, and given an unnecessary build-up? Have I piled on too much detail, so that none is memorable or salient? Have I left the scene as quickly as possible, or dragged it out?

It may be useful to consider the approach of scriptwriters. They understand scenes in terms of 'the hook', which is an action or piece of dialogue at the start, and 'the tag', which may sum up the scene, mark a turn or twist in the plot, reveal a new aspect of character, or point to what follows.

summaries

When writers rewrite they often cut scenes that don't add to or support their intentions. They might also decide that some scenes should be summaries, which are short passages of exposition that convey information quickly. Unlike scenes, they provide information by *telling*. They describe, explain, clarify, interpret, link scenes and help guide the reader through the stages of a story or novel. They may cover a long period of time, or convey a large amount of information that would normally require many scenes. Here is an example from David Malouf's short story, 'Bad Blood':

> They had a child as well, a little girl just like the mother, and Alice didn't know how to look after the baby either. She didn't change its nappies or keep it clean. It was always hungry, dirty, crawling about the unswept floor covered with flies. Uncle Jake was distracted. At last he stopped going to

work—there were no more fresh little rolls, no more green iced frogs with open mouths. He stayed home to care for the child, while Alice, as lazy and beautiful as ever, just sat about reading *Photoplay* till he lost his temper and blacked her eye. Uncle Jake doted on the child but felt dismayed, un-manned. He fretted for his old life of careless independence.

As an exercise, rework the above as two or three scenes.

A well-paced work of fiction will achieve a fine balance between the 'highs' of the scenes and the 'lows' of the summaries.

transitions

How do you move a character from A to B, or from one stage of a story or novel to the next? Generally, if important events occur at both A and B, then trivial details like riding between the two points in a lift or taxi can be omitted.

Transitions should be smooth and effortless, and the next stage a suitable one, suggested by what has preceded it. If Olivia slams the door after telling Jack, 'I've had it with you, I'm finding somewhere else to live', then the next time we meet her she should be living elsewhere, not still with Jack (unless the point is that she's always threatening to leave and never does).

The actual transition can be indicated by: a new chapter in a novel; a 'time-lapse space' (a small gap between blocks of printed text); a typographical device such as a row of asterisks; a simple transitional phrase ('When Jack got home at six he discovered that...'); a transitional passage (for example, after Olivia announces that she's leaving Jack she can be placed in a taxi on her way to her new place, thinking over her next moves or starting to regret what she's done. A transition of this kind can be effective if the action at A and B is so intense that it needs relief.

In general the purpose of a transition is to move forward in time or to a new location, or introduce a new action or character.

flashbacks

Flashbacks are used to bring in key background information from an earlier time. They are usually in the nature of a remembered scene, related in speech, or reported in the narrative. The word 'had' need only be used two or three times at the beginning of the flashback passage to establish a movement into the past.

Flashbacks work best in novels. They are apt to weaken the flow and spoil the focus of shorter short stories. Avoid using flashbacks at critical stages of stories and novels for fear of defusing tension, or too early, for fear of 'backgrounding' story and characters before readers have had a chance to establish what the foreground is.

Also, it's often possible to convey the same information more naturally and seamlessly in a brief thought or passage of dialogue. But, if unavoidable, flashbacks should be concise, economical and to the point

children's picture-books

The writers of picture-books need to take into account not only the role of the illustrations in conveying story and characterisation but also the constraints of technology. Owing to the way picture-books are printed, there are only 32 pages on which to arrange the text and the illustrations. If the first three pages are set aside for the half-title page, publisher's imprint page and main title page, there are only 29 pages left. Although the designer, editor and illustrator work together as a team to plan the layout of the book once the text has been written, it can help picture-book writers to 'map out' the text in 29 (or fewer, as necessary) blocks of text, bearing in mind that the illustrations won't simply reflect the text but will *expand* upon it. It's important, therefore, to cut redundancies, repetitions and qualifiers, trusting the illustrator to 'fill in the gaps'. Creating suspense and tension—the need in the reader to turn the page—is as important in picture-books as longer works of fiction. A question or issue might best be posed on the right-hand page and answered *over* the page, for example, rather than be asked and answered on a double spread. It can take months to write a picture-book of only two or three hundred words.

ten

SETTING

My task is to make you hear, to make you feel,
to make you see.
JOSEPH CONRAD

The setting is where the action of a story or novel takes place. I believe that beginner writers often don't understand how vital it is, and will simply tack it on to locate characters and action. In fact, setting is indivisible from the other elements of fiction, such as character, plot and point of view, and will enhance a story or novel by way of its atmosphere and relationship to the characters. It may even be, as in Liam Davison's novel, *Soundings*, a central or controlling element. Davison's characters become obsessed with the landscape of Westernport in Victoria as they variously explore, settle and photograph it.

Setting should never be taken for granted. By selecting and highlighting aspects of the setting, and using the power of words to evoke atmospheres and sensations, writers can bring readers closer to the action and provoke responses in them.

Some novels and stories are unimaginable without their settings or in alternative settings: the small towns and farms of southern Ontario in the short stories of Alice Munro, for example, the Texas/Mexico border country in the novels of Cormac McCarthy, the Louisiana bayous of James Lee Burke's crime novels, the grasslands and imagined landscapes of Gerald Murnane, Martin Amis's London and the inner-city suburbs of Helen Garner. In each case the setting influences not only characters, actions and milieu but also tone and style. For example, Burke's characters and language are dark and sultry, in keeping with the steamy landscape.

ELEMENTS OF THE SETTING

A setting is composed of one or more of the following elements:

- objects: e.g. trees, clouds, motor cars, tables, chairs, ashtrays
- people: e.g. a newspaper boy shouting out on a street corner; a child creating a cubbyhole out of chairs and cushions
- ambience: e.g. sounds, shapes, colours, odours, the quality of the light, aspects of the climate
- atmosphere: e.g. menacing, joyful, gloomy, tense.

CHARACTERS AND SETTING

When reading a novel or story that impresses you with its evocation of place and atmosphere, note the close relationship between characters and setting. Not only are characters a part of the setting, they influence, respond to and are informed by it. Skilful fiction writers can evoke settings in such a way as to signify the feelings and personalities of their characters. 'Stalking', a short story by the American writer Joyce Carol

Oates, is set in a modern American shopping centre with its hard, bright, sharp surfaces and colours, neon signs, asphalt parking lot and exhaust fumes. This setting, and the way it's described, create an alienating, disturbing, off-balance atmosphere in keeping with the moods and fantasies of the main character, an unhappy adolescent.

The setting of 'Stalking' is appropriate in terms of character and theme. Writers also use *contrast* to good effect: for example, by showing a depressed character in a field of daisies on a spring day.

Always ask yourself who is viewing the setting at any point. If it's you, the author, then ask yourself how neutral or responsive you should be, or how remote or intimate, for this will decide the words you'll use and how you'll use them. It's possible to describe a city slum with disgust, for example, or with a neutral gaze. The same applies to settings seen from the point of view of your fictional characters. A fastidious character might recoil from a city slum, a character in a buoyant mood see something positive in it, a hardened police officer feel cynical toward it.

It helps if you can encourage readers to respond to the setting as your characters do. A scene in which a fearful character walks through a spooky graveyard at midnight is going to have little impact unless the reader also feels fearful.

EVOKING THE SETTING

appeal to the five senses

Stories and novels (and non-fiction, such as travel books) are vivid and easier to appreciate when readers are encouraged to touch, hear, see, smell and taste aspects of the setting. Compare these two passages:

'I knelt and touched his face. It was clear that he was dead.'

'I knelt and touched his cheek. It was cold, waxy. The guy was dead.'

In the second passage readers are invited to imagine what it would be like to *touch* a dead man's face. They are brought into the scene, closer to the action, and encouraged to respond along with the narrator; the sensual detail evokes a more imaginable, and therefore vivid, picture. But note, too, the clipped, abrupt *style*: it adds to the intended effect, and helps characterise the narrator. It's not unusual for more than one effect to be at work in a passage of writing.

Here the other senses are engaged:

sound

'He pulled his foot free of the mud with a sound like the tearing of a cotton sheet.' The reader is being asked to hear a specific and recognisable sound in this sentence. Another important writers' tip is also operating here: *it's better to be specific than general*. The writer might have written 'with a sharp sound', but there are many kinds of sharp sound; the 'tearing of a cotton sheet' is a much more precise description.

smell

'Anna bent her head to his little neck, closed her eyes and breathed deeply of the talc, the freshly laundered blanket, his milky skin.' This is better than 'Anna breathed in his baby smells', for it's specific, tells us something about Anna and shows her reacting to her environment.

sight

'Just across the field from us was an oak forest, no more than a grey smudge in the endless slanting rain.' This tells the reader what the scene looks like, and also gives information about light quality and air temperature. It appeals to other senses as well as sight: one can almost hear, smell and touch this scene.

taste

Taste is not often evoked in fiction (unless the subject is food), but, like smell, taste is one of the most powerful senses. A windy beach scene would be more vivid if readers could taste the salt spray, for example.

Sometimes a particularised *absence* of sensory details can be effective; for example, to emphasise the barrenness of a landscape.

A useful exercise for new writers attempting to develop their powers of observation is to follow the advice of Dorothea Brande, as given in her writers' handbook, *Becoming a Writer*: 'turn yourself into a stranger in your own street'. In other words, take nothing for granted but view a familiar setting with fresh eyes.

create an appropriate atmosphere

By skilful manipulation of the setting, writers can enhance the atmosphere of a scene (or even an entire book) or the circumstances of a character. Note the air of creeping menace in Thomas Harris's serial killer crime novel, *The Silence of the Lambs*, and of claustrophobia in Magnus Mills's darkly comic novel, *The Restraint of Beasts*, in which a trio of workmen find themselves trapped in a small rural community.

be selective

Try to be selective when describing a scene, providing only those details that suit the main intention behind it.

For example, to show a character finding solace in a cathedral you might note the soft golden candlesticks, warm wooden pews, sunlight streaming through the stained-glass windows and reverence of the worshippers. To show that character failing to find solace you'd highlight other aspects of the cathedral or describe the same ones in different ways: the cold slate floors, for example, the hardness of the pews, the gloomy shadows. To make a job interview seem intimidating a writer might describe the interviewers ranged intimidatingly behind a large table in a stark room, rather than the bright carpet and paintings, the friendly secretary or the smell of freshly brewed coffee—unless the intention is to set up false expectations in the reader and the interviewee.

imply and simplify

A brief sketch will often be more effective than a long description. Certainly short stories should not be mired with long setting descriptions, for these may destroy the atmosphere or slow the pace. It can be sufficient to focus on one telling detail: red wine pooling on a white tablecloth will have a particular reverberation in a scene where two lovers quarrel bitterly.

Long descriptive passages are usually intended, particularly in novels, to have a particular logic, momentum, tone or structure; that is, to do a certain job. In Charles Frazier's *Cold Mountain* an American Civil War deserter journeys far through a rugged, unfamiliar, sparsely populated landscape, dodging treacherous locals and gangs of other deserters. He is on foot. The journey takes months. Inevitably he is consumed by the landscape as it offers dangers, obstacles and opportunities for contemplation and appreciation.

SYMBOLS

An emblem of the setting, if repeated, can also act as a symbol. For example, a family lives in a house in which there are three china figurines on a mantelpiece, representing the moral precepts 'See no evil, hear no evil, speak no evil'. These figurines might be used by the writer to symbolise the actions or hypocrisies of the family members. Washing left on a line for several weeks might symbolise half-measures or carelessness.

FORESHADOWING

An aspect of the setting can be selected and elaborated on in a short story or novel until it attains a significance in keeping with the theme or action of a story. A novel might have a panoramic opening in which there's a town and a dam with a mossy bank. Throughout the novel townspeople fish from the bank, or picnic on it, or lovers meet there. It might get dry and cracked during a drought and symbolise a character's reversal of fortune. Finally, it might collapse in a flood at the crisis point of the story—an event foreshadowed at the opening and throughout the novel. Although a useful device, foreshadowing should be subtle, and relevant to the main point of a story or novel. See it as 'sowing seeds of prediction'.

SIMILES AND METAPHORS

Similes and metaphors are figures of speech. In the case of the simile, two things or actions are likened to each other (usually with the words 'like' or 'as'), either for clarity or ease of explanation or for rhetorical or poetic effect: for example, 'Oak trees showed on the misty hillsides *like* smudges of smoke'. The metaphor can be understood as a vivid extension of the simile in the sense that a word or descriptive term is applied to something to which it is not literally applicable: for example, 'The oak trees *were* smudges of smoke on the misty hillsides'. Arresting, accurate and appropriate similes and metaphors can help readers imagine settings clearly and economically. Those that are over-used, exaggerated or miss the target can be greatly distracting.

THE WORDS ON THE PAGE

Chapter 13 discusses effective style in greater detail, but I wish to make the point that good fiction writers work like poets when they describe settings. They pay attention not only to meanings of words but also to sound, rhythm and imagery. In the following passage, the long 'o' sounds of the first sentence suggest the slow, heaving motion of the open sea:

> A night on the sea in an open boat is a long night. As darkness finally settled, the shine of the light, lifting from the sea in the south, changed to full gold. On the northern horizon a new light appeared, a small bluish gleam on the edge of the waters. These two lights were the furniture of the world. Otherwise there was nothing but the waves.
>
> (Stephen Crane, 'The Open Boat')

FAMILIAR PLACES

If you're familiar with an actual place then it's only natural that you'd want to use it in a story or novel. For readers, familiarity with a setting can be a powerful element in the appeal of a work of fiction, because they can be there with the characters.

Sometimes you'll give yourself the creative licence to alter aspects of the setting so that a detail of your plot can work better; at other times you'll want to be accurate (readers of my crime novels are quick to correct me if I write that a certain street is one-way east to west when it should be west to east).

You might also discover, as Liam Davison did when he went back to the French village in which he'd set his novel, *The Betrayal*, that your fictionalised place is more 'real' and interesting than the actual place:

Now, while you're standing there lost and dislocated, trying to reconcile the place you see with the place you know, ask yourself which one's more real. Which one is wrong? If you can confidently say that the fictional world you have created has more validity than the place you see, you can rest assured that your fiction is well grounded. Your job is not to report the world as others see it but to re-create it. Ultimately, the fiction writer's responsibility is to the fiction, and setting or sense of place is an integral part of it. It should never be mistaken for the factual recounting of a real place or for a scenic backdrop against which your dramatic action unfolds.

OTHER WORLDS AND TIMES

It's a rule of thumb that you should 'write about what you know'. When I wrote *The Divine Wind*, which deals in part with the Japanese bombing of the remote pearling town of Broome on the north-west coast of Australia in early 1942, I had never been to Broome and was born some time after the Second World War. But I didn't feel that these factors were an impediment to me as a writer. I knew something about human nature, after all, and research handled the rest. I read travel books published in the 1930s, together with histories of Broome, the pearling industry and the Japanese air-raids, and examined old photographs. They were sufficient for me to be able to step inside a character from that era and walk through the landscape with him. In other words, I used historical details imaginatively and suggestively, and to give a sense of verisimilitude, but was careful not to overload the novel with historical details and so lose sight of the characters and their problems.

When writers set their novels in the past, they try to give an impression of the moral atmosphere along with the historical. For example, through the figure of Charles Darwin's manservant, Syms Covington, in *Mr Darwin's Shooter*, Roger McDonald is able to dramatise the conflict between science and religion in the nineteenth century.

Writers of science fiction also use techniques of suggestion to evoke other or alternative worlds. They know that too much esoteric, technical or unfamiliar detail will obscure the story.

eleven

WRITING A SHORT STORY

> *As we read Chekhov's little stories about nothing at*
> *all, the horizon widens.*
> VIRGINIA WOOLF

Short stories are generally undervalued. New writers treat them as warm-up exercises for the novel, English teachers find them convenient for filling a lesson, there are few publishing opportunities for them, and the form is misunderstood. In this chapter, I want to make a case for the complexity and richness of the short story.

THIS IS NOT A SHORT STORY

I once asked my fellow writing students at Stanford University to workshop a short piece I'd written based on a friend's rueful recollection of the day he'd picked up a male hitchhiker and endured an uncomfortable journey because the man had been accompanied by two large dogs which my friend had initially mistaken for a couple of backpacks.

'This is amusing,' they said, 'but it's an anecdote, not a short story.'

Of the many thousands of stories I've read as a teacher and competition judge over the years, a significant number were anecdotes, sketches, vignettes, mood pieces, tracts, doggerel and little flashes on life. Like my Stanford piece, they were short, but they weren't short stories. They were unsatisfying, for they lacked the complexity, movement, consequence and subtle contrivance of the unexpected and the marvellous that we regard as fundamental to storytelling. I later rewrote the Stanford story, changing the hitchhiker to a young woman and thereby introducing an element of sexual tension, which acts as a dark undercurrent in counterpoint to the humour of the original situation. It was later published and won a short-story award.

A SHORT HISTORY OF THE SHORT STORY

How has the short story been understood over the years? In the nineteenth century, Edgar Allan Poe said that it should have 'unity of impression'. Most stories of the pre-modernist era are objective, straightforward, realistic narratives with clearly defined themes. Then, toward the end of the century, writers like Anton Chekhov began to pay less attention to plot and more to other kinds of shift or movement—of mood and insight, for example. At the turn of the century, O. Henry popularised the surprise ending, the twist in the tail. Jeffrey Archer, and thousands of beginner writers, continue to have faith in that model.

In the modern era of the early twentieth century, the short story moved toward a more metaphoric, symbolic and ironic presentation, as well as a modified realism. Freudian theory, scientific discoveries, industrialisation and mass society influenced writers like Virginia Woolf and Franz Kafka. Then James Joyce defined stories in terms of the epiphany—the revelation (for protagonist and reader) which occurs toward the end of the story.

The short-story writing courses and writers' handbooks that blossomed in the US in the 1950s set out certain conventions:

- stories should be neatly made, with believable characters, a storyline, and a theme
- stories should work through suggestion and compression to create points of illumination
- show, don't tell
- cultivate understatement
- keep the narrative voice distinct from those of your characters
- develop a central image or symbol to convey your theme objectively
- point everything toward a neatly sprung ironic reversal.

Then in the 1960s there was a major reaction to the traditional story. One American writer, Grace Paley, rejected plot in these words: 'I've always despised plot, the absolute line between two points, because it takes all hope away.' She also rejected the closed ending, which crushed her characters, in favour of the *apparently* unstructured sort that permitted her characters 'the open destiny of life'.

American writers like Robert Coover, Donald Barthelme and Richard Brautigan began to use myth, fantasy and dream in their short stories. They paid more attention to language and the creative process itself than to character, theme, and storyline. Their stories were apparently plotless, and had no obvious point, meaning or resolution. They dispelled order and unity and explained nothing. They often took extreme, offensive or absurd positions. Questions weren't answered or even posed. Characters were ruled by chance, coincidence and chaos, had experiences that contradicted our own, and didn't resemble anyone we knew, from our middle range of experience.

This movement delivered a sorely needed breath of fresh air to short-story writing and its effect is still noticeable. Fashions change. The next major movement from the United States was 'dirty realism', which took as its subject matter the modest expectations and disappointments of small town, blue collar men and women. Richard Ford, Raymond Carver, Tobias Wolff and Bobbie Ann Mason were very influential and greatly admired for their stories, and I confess that they are amongst my favourite writers, but I can see some truth in this blistering attack from the short-story writer and critic, Mark Helprin:

> Why are so many of these stories about despicable people in filthy apartments filled with ugly bric-a-brac, where everyone smokes, drinks, stays up all night, and is addicted to coffee? Why are the characters uniformly pudgy, stiff and out of shape? Why do they watch so much television? Why are their lives inextricably intertwined with brand names? Why is their hair dirty? Why don't they work at a profession or a trade? What are they doing in university towns in their middle age? Why do they seem to exist as if there were no landscape? Why are they never in love or involved in something that scares the death out of them?

In more recent years we've become interested in stories that not only treat a subject or distil an experience but also say something about the form of the story. We've also become interested in the three competing fields of: the author's intentions, the reader's responses, and the cultural grounds of the subject itself.

DEFINING CHARACTERISTICS OF TRADITIONAL SHORT STORIES

shortness

That a short story is short might seem obvious, but I'm often asked, 'How long should a short story be?'

Unfortunately the marketplace tends to give writers a fixed impression of story length: competitions with their 3000-word upper limit, for example, and the tendency of little magazines to favour short over long stories owing to space considerations.

The only reasonable answer to the above question is, 'Don't think about length until it's time to market a story. A story is as long as it needs to be to complete the task at hand.' That said, it's worth noting certain tendencies: short-short stories are about 1000 words long (Colette's 'The Other Wife' is a wonderful example of the complexity and density that can be accomplished in so few words); competition and little-magazine stories are between 2000 and 5000 words long; and some authors and readers enjoy the relative expansiveness of the *long* story of up to 15000 words (see *The Granta Book of the American Long Story*, edited by Richard Ford). The question of how the long story differs from the novella (a short-short novel) is open to debate, but I urge you to read E. Annie

Proulx's *Brokeback Mountain*, which was first published as a short story in a magazine, then in book form as a novella, and finally in her short-story collection, *Close Range*. It's evocative, moving and powerful whether you call it a short story or long story or novella.

Conventionally, a short novel has 30000 to 40000 words, romance novels about 50000, and ordinary novels about 50000–70000 words or more.

treatment of characters

Compared to novels, short stories tend to have few characters and explore one aspect of personality rather than personality in depth.

settings

Short stories tend to have few, if any, changes of setting.

time scale

Short stories tend to cover relatively short periods of time: an hour in the case of Colette's 'The Other Wife'.

density

Although the longer stories of short-story writers such as Alice Munro, Richard Ford, William Trevor and Edna O'Brien have the density of many novels, short stories generally stay within the worlds they have established, stick to the point and avoid tangents.

economy

In the short story only the essentials exist. There are no repetitions, lengthy descriptions, extended passages of dialogue, wasted characters or extraneous scenes. The writer uses implication, careful selection and compression to achieve the required effect. The 1000 words of Colette's 'The Other Wife' are so efficient that they do the job of a 50000-word novel.

Of course, these characteristics may also apply to novels— Howard Norman's *The Museum Guard*, for example, is closely focused, has few characters and settings, and covers a relatively brief period of time—but novels generally have the capacity to cover large ground.

A STORY AT WORK

Here is a short story, followed by an analysis of it. Given that the approach is conventional, it may not be the type of story you'd normally write or choose to read, so treat it as a useful starting point to understanding how short stories work. One of the best ways to gain a sense of the rich variety of story-telling modes is to read the many short-story anthologies, often collected by theme, that are available (see Further Reading).

Restoration

She waited for him outside the British Institute Library. She was on time. When he had not arrived after ten minutes she imagined the teasing she would give him. Forty minutes later she knew that she was at fault. She looked at the list of tenants in the building's foyer. She stood on the footpath, opened her map, looked both ways along the Lungarno. Hot, mutely desperate tourists toiled by. Taxis and three-wheeled vans fumed and braked on the street and young locals howled through the gaps on mopeds, elbows out and limbs flying like rakish insects. The heat and the racket drove her back into the foyer. She had not been to Europe before.

Evan said, when he found her: 'The British Institute, Anne, not the Institute Library. Over there, look.' He pointed to the other side of the river. 'I showed it to you yesterday. Never mind, I've found you now. We go down here,' he said, striding off. 'What did you do today?'

He had his sketches with him, in a leather slip-case under his arm. Anne hurried beside and occasionally behind him along side streets and across Piazza San Spirito. 'I went to the Uffizi,' she called, at one point.

'Down here,' he said.

They emerged onto Via Maggio and walked south, away from the river.

'I saw the restored *Venus*.'

He turned around and waited for her. 'It looks like a glossy poster, don't you think? They should never have restored it. We cross over here.'

When they were on the other side of the street she reached forward, gripped his elbow and pointed to a wedge-shaped building across from them. 'I came past here today. That's where the Brownings lived.'

Evan said, 'Uh huh' and hurried her along the street.

She said, 'I stumbled on it quite by chance.' She'd been in the city for three days now and her head and her heart were brimming.

'Down here,' Evan said.

They entered a small street and he paused to peer at a brass plate of tenants' call-buttons fastened to the stone wall next to a heavy wooden door. He was interrupted by a girl who ran in from Via Maggio and flung herself at the buttons. She wore bright, stylish clothes and bobbed giddily before the fretwork of the speaker.

The speaker crackled into life: '*Si?*'

'*Sono Piera!*'

'*Ciao! Sali!*'

The electric lock disengaged and the girl plunged through the door. Anne glimpsed marble stairs and flashing heels before the door swung crisply shut with a sound weighted with age and privilege.

Then Evan put his finger to the button.

'Hello?'

'It's Evan.'

'Darling. Come on up.'

They entered the building and climbed through cool, muted light. 'Darling, is it?' said Anne.

'She's sixty, for Christ's sake.'

'Evan. I was only teasing.'

They turned at a landing and climbed again. 'That girl who came in,' Anne said. 'Everyone's so beautifully dressed here.'

'Yes, well,' Evan said, and on the third floor he knocked on a door and seemed to pace on the spot.

Eventually a voice called, 'Come,' but then the door was opened for them.

'Dear boy.'

A tall, angular woman clasped Evan's shoulders and kissed his cheeks in the local manner. She was erect, unequivocal. 'And this must be your friend,' she said.

'This is Anne.'

'Anne. Of course. Evan informs me you've not seen one another for some time. We here are very proud of him, you know.'

Anne was held and kissed and had no opportunity to answer the woman. 'Anne, this is Mrs Peterhouse,' Evan said.

'Margaret,' said Mrs Peterhouse, leading them across the tiled hallway of her apartment. 'Come through, won't you? Hugh's here already.'

She glanced at Evan's slip-case. 'I see you've been working, dear boy.'

Evan stopped and took out a sheaf of small canvases and watercolours. 'I thought I'd show these to Hugh.'

'*What* a good idea.'

Anne lingered as they walked on. She bent swiftly to run her hand over the floor tiles. They were cool and uneven, worn smooth like the tiles in the floor of a church. Church: *chiesa*, she corrected herself sternly.

She looked around. Mrs Peterhouse had money, that much was clear. According to Evan she also owned a villa near Siena and a house in London and thought nothing of going from one to the other. She liked to introduce painters to writers and musicians to photographers, and would buy their works and invite them for drinks.

Drinkies, Anne thought.

'Here we are,' Mrs Peterhouse was saying, 'be it ever so humble. Anne, dear, I should like you to meet...,' and Anne shook various hands. She understood that Susannah was nineteen and Mrs Peterhouse's god-daughter, and Lorenzo some kind of count. Susannah announced ringingly that she was leaving Italy after two weeks as a nanny and certain infuriating experiences—which perhaps accounted for her offended air. Lorenzo was elegant, corrupt, delicately boned. He briefly touched his fingers to Anne's, established that she was not English, and turned back to Susannah, whose nose was tilted above his gleaming head.

And so Anne stood adrift in the vast room, holding a glass of gin and tonic and wondering when she might reasonably interrupt Evan. Evan was hovering in an attitude of delightful anxiety on the stone hearth of the fireplace, passing his paintings one by one to Hugh Lovatt, who sat in an ancient oak and leather chair. Lovatt had a tartar's face, encouraged by wings of white hair and a red kerchief at his neck. His arms and hands were brown and veined. One knuckle was flecked with yellow paint. He had not removed his beret and what he said counted.

At that moment, unwitnessed by Evan, an expression of fatigue and outrage passed over Lovatt's face. Anne walked across to them.

Evan saw her, but half-turned his back on her, and she heard him say, 'This is the same tabernacle but with the sun drenching it. Actually there were dead flowers in it that day but I needed the red to offset this rusty colour.' He leaned down and pointed.

Hugh Lovatt shifted in the chair. After a while he said tightly, 'Well judged.'

Anne waited. Evan showed surprise. 'There you are. I was just showing Hugh my tabernacle series.'

Lovatt stood and took both of her hands and glittered at her.

'Hugh, this is Anne, the friend I was telling you about.'

'Friend,' breathed Lovatt, gripping her hands.

Anne exchanged smiles with Lovatt for an extended period. She said, half-desperately, 'Evan says you're having a retrospective exhibition in Melbourne soon. Have you really not been back for fifteen years?'

'More,' said Lovatt abruptly. He released her. Then he brightened again and put an arm around Evan's shoulders. 'What do you think of our boy here? What a champion, eh?'

They each laughed a little uncontrollably and Evan said, 'And what are you working on at the moment, Hugh?'

'Now, now,' said Lovatt, shaking his head.

He turned to regard Anne. He held up a finger. 'There's something you really must see,' he said. 'I want to borrow your *friend* for just a moment, all right, champion?' He walked her across and out of the room. 'Such a...productive boy.'

Anne found herself in Mrs Peterhouse's library. 'Over here,' Lovatt said, 'over here.' He stopped. 'There.'

Anne leaned into a dark space between glass-fronted cabinets. 'Is it a Turner?'

'A Turner. Yes. On the knocker. Right first time.'

Lovatt rocked on his heels and pursed his lips at the painting. Finally Anne said, 'I love Turner.'

'Don't we all, sweetie, don't we all. What a dear girl.'

'I read on the plane over here that he'd painted in Italy.'

'And this,' said Lovatt, 'is one of them.'

They stood marvelling and the seconds passed by. Anne said, 'Evan told me you're giving a lecture on Turner.'

'Tomorrow afternoon, yes.'

'We were thinking of going.'

'Lovely,' said Lovatt. He lowered his voice elaborately. 'But bear in mind as you listen—they're just a bit Women's Institutish here in Florence, if you get my drift.'

Before she could stop herself Anne said, 'It must get you down needing to give lectures when you'd rather just paint. Evan says...'

'Quite,' said Lovatt, turning on his heel.

Anne trailed behind him back to Mrs Peterhouse's living room, her heart beating.

'Has he been showing you my little treasure?' Mrs Peterhouse cried.

Anne told her how beautiful the Turner was. By now everyone was standing together at the broad windows, watching the transfiguring light and shadows in a corner of the Boboli Gardens. It was half-past seven. Anne sipped her drink. 'Today I saw the restored *Venus*,' she said.

'Did you? I've not seen it,' Mrs Peterhouse said.

'I couldn't take my eyes...'

At her side, Evan made a jovial gesture. He said, 'We should think about dinner. Is anyone interested in having a bite somewhere?'

'What is your impression, Hugh?' said Mrs Peterhouse.

'Of what—the *Venus* or dinner with the champ?'

'The *Venus*.'

'I intend,' said Lovatt, 'to preserve the impressions of my youth. I expect they've turned it into some kind of glossy poster.'

Anne looked at Susannah and Lorenzo and understood that she could take the subject no further. Lorenzo was finding Susannah's indifference attractive. Susannah, now meeting his eye from time to time, was exercising it for all she was worth.

Evan said, 'Do you know of a good *trattoria* near here, Margaret?'

But Mrs Peterhouse was saying, 'Why, Hugh, what a marvellous idea for a lecture: the artist as a young man. What it meant to you to come to Italy. The influences. Do you think you could bear to talk to us again, possibly later in the year?'

Lovatt looked down at his wine glass as upon something that had begun to warm his heart. 'Oh, I dare say I could fit you in,' he said.

'Splendid. I'll arrange it with the Director.'

Everyone moved about agreeably. Evan, for one, would be keen to compare his own experiences with Hugh's.

'Then it's all settled,' Mrs Peterhouse said.

Some time later, when they were crossing the Ponte Vecchio, Anne said to Evan, 'There's no rush. Let's stop for a minute.'

She leaned on the parapet of the bridge and looked out across the river, at the dark surface speckled with reflected light. Behind her couples were strolling arm in arm and she could hear murmurs and soft throaty laughter and the music of a moonlit night.

Evan said, as he joined her, 'Or I could make an omelette. There should be a few eggs left.'

'Evan.' Anne raised and dropped her hands. 'I want to go to a *trattoria*. My treat.'

Evan looked hunted. 'Which one? I don't know what any of these places are like.'

Anne stared at him. He stood unquiet, prudish, agitated at her side, and looked at but possibly did not see the river or the city. Panic and longing still drove him. The year here had not solved that.

His miscalculations dismayed Anne. What was he doing with fakes and snobs and Anglophile Italians, not a one of them redeemed by intellect? Or with his finger still in a phrase-book? She had come this far—if she were to stay then he must start to admit some risk and improvisation into their lives.

'Choose,' she said.

ANALYSIS

shape

'Restoration' has a classic short-story shape—a gradual build-up to a crisis point, followed by a rapid falling-off.

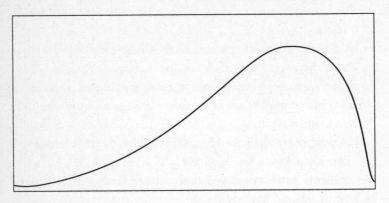

The main stages are:

initiating incident

Anne, the main character, overseas for the first time, makes a simple mistake for which she is rebuked by her lover, Evan, whom she has not seen for twelve months. The incident gives a brief glimpse into their personalities and is both a symptom of their relationship in the past and indicative of what might happen later in the story. It would be a mistake for the story to give too much away at this stage.

complication and conflict

Evan is increasingly distant and agitated (and we learn why later). Anne is cheerful, optimistic and curious about the world around her, but she finds no answering spark in Evan.

rising action

Evan is desperate to impress the wealthy art collector, Mrs Peterhouse, and the famous artist, Hugh Lovatt. Anne, overlooked by everyone, begins to see unpleasant qualities in Evan, Mrs Peterhouse and Hugh Lovatt.

crisis

The story comes to a head when Evan tries unsuccessfully to get a dinner party together and Anne to convey her delight in a famous painting. Anne and Evan are sidelined by the others but the real 'victim' is Anne. In effect, Evan has betrayed her. He continues to seek approval from the others and, like them, is too self-absorbed to care that Anne has been moved by the beauty of a painting. In a sense, everyone but Anne is blind to the real beauty in things.

(Of course, this theme is often found in fiction. See, for example, Katherine Mansfield's short story, 'The Doll's House'.)

falling action

Anne finds herself alone with Evan, who is disappointed and ineffectual. She begins to reassess her relationship with him.

dénouement

Anne has certain expectations, and has invested a lot; the rest is up to Evan now.

length

At about 2000 words, 'Restoration' meets the length requirements of most competitions and little magazines.

characterisation

This is developed through dialogue, thoughts and actions. We are closest to Anne. We not only see and hear her, we know what she is thinking. Our impressions of the other characters change as she begins to see other sides to them. But we trust her; she is intelligent, observant and perceptive, without being too judgemental. The minor characters, Mrs Peterhouse and Hugh Lovatt, are developed only to the extent that they make clearer to us aspects of Anne's lover, Evan.

conflict

This can be seen in terms of a character (Anne) with a governing personality characteristic (generosity of spirit), faced with a troubling situation (her lover, whom she has not seen for some time, is giving all of his attention to a circle of shallow acquaintances). Her generosity of spirit is tested by the situation and she must weigh her self-regard against her loyalty to a relationship. And there are secondary complications too, related to the main one: she's taken for granted by the others, her views are not treated seriously, and she's seen as an appendage to Evan.

dialogue

Dialogue is used to reveal moods, attitudes and character traits, give information to the reader in a natural-sounding way, and dramatise moments when the characters are awkward with or misunderstand one another. Have a look at the way Hugh Lovatt curtly interrupts Anne when she unsuspectingly alludes to the fact that he is a has-been or feels that he might be one.

setting

In the opening paragraph Anne begins to feel stranded and anxious and so the setting is appropriately hectic and confusing. In the later scenes she is curious and appreciative, but the people she meets stand in unfortunate contrast to their gracious surroundings. This is especially marked in the final scene when Evan seems blind to the beauty of the city and the river.

point of view

'Restoration' is told in the limited third-person point of view, and so the reader advances into the story through the perceptions of one character only: Anne. We don't know what is said or done in Mrs Peterhouse's apartment when Anne is not there, or what any of the other characters feel or think, although Anne may speculate about these things. The first-person point of view would have achieved the same effect but, owing to its greater intimacy, have seemed too stifling in such a contained situation, and detracted from the evocation of place. Of course, a more omniscient third-person point of view, taking us into the viewpoints of several characters or a God-like narrator, would have spoilt the tension and focus in a story as short as this.

implication

Our information is filtered through Anne, but Anne is an observant, sensitive witness and we sense, along with her, what lies 'between the lines'. For example, when we watch Hugh Lovatt through her eyes we see that he is humouring Evan. The reader is encouraged to receive impressions and speculate about characters rather than be a passive receptor.

beginning

'Restoration' starts quickly, at an advanced stage of the story. We don't need to see Anne flying to Europe, or arriving at the airport, and since there are several allusions to Anne's and Evan's past together, no need for a flashback.

ending

One episode in the relationship between Anne and Evan has closed and a new one is about to begin. It's possible that Evan will never change, but Anne is ready to give him a chance. She's had her eyes opened; she's not prepared to let things go on as they have been, but the change, the effort, must come from Evan. 'Choose,' she says, and means more than simply which restaurant.

title

The word 'restoration' applies to the restored painting in the gallery that so affected Anne, but it also applies to the theme of the story: Can, or should, the relationship between Anne and Evan be restored?

theme

'Restoration' is a story about the loss of innocence or, alternatively, the getting of wisdom. Without this element, the events—a young woman goes to Florence to be with her boyfriend and meets some oddball characters—would merely be anecdotal.

final points

'Restoration' has a unity of impression, with no digressions or wasted characters and scenes and everything contributing to the story. It reveals its secrets slowly and shows that a short story need not be full of action; the events and their consequences may simply reveal a subtle shift. It's not a novel and so a deep development of character, background and setting would have been inappropriate. The contrasts, such as between talent and mediocrity, refinement and vulgarity, sophistication and gaucherie, Anglo-Saxon reserve and Italian vivacity, relate to the main point of the story. Finally, the story's energy grows out of the tension between three conflicting forces: Anne, Evan, and the world of Mrs Peterhouse and Hugh Lovatt. If one of the three had been missing, the story might have failed.

1. Try rewriting 'Restoration' from Evan's viewpoint. How does the story's focus change?
2. Imagine that 'Restoration' is part of a discontinuous narrative. Write another story for it: for example, Evan before he travels overseas; the inner life of Hugh Lovatt; Susannah baby-sitting the daughter of a wealthy Florentine family.
3. Rewrite the story so that Evan has blossomed from his time in Florence and Anne is blind to the beauties and possibilities of the city.

4. Do a similar exercise of analysis on short stories you have been reading, and try to see what makes them work well, or fail in some way.

MAKING A STORY LONGER

There is something satisfying about the *long* short story. It's my preferred form, and I fell into it by chance, so to speak, after spending several months and tens of thousands of words on novels that should only have been longish short stories. Rewritten as stories, they worked and readily found publication. Alice Munro once said, of writing her long stories: 'I can get a kind of tension when I'm writing a short story, like I'm pulling on a rope and I know where the rope is attached. With a novel, everything goes flabby.'

But first I should point out that most short stories benefit from *cutting*: characters, incidents, sub-plots, long descriptions, slow beginnings, drawn-out endings, windy dialogue, repetitions, indulgences and overkill—in fact, anything that doesn't advance the story or rattles when you shake the pages.

So when could or should a story be longer? Sometimes aspects of a writer's personal life can be a factor. For example, Raymond Carver was battling alcoholism and poverty when he wrote his brief, fleeting, disturbing short story, 'The Bath'. He once described his early writing methods as 'Get in. Get out. Don't linger'. Later he found a measure of happiness in his life, and as his stories grew longer, with greater emotional depth and a widening range of images, gestures and tones, he rewrote 'The Bath'. Titled 'A Small Good Thing', it's more than three times longer than 'The Bath', and full of the possibilities of grace and forgiveness. But most under-developed short stories are usually full of missed opportunities. Here are some ways in which you might expand a story— first asking yourself if it *needs* expanding, of course, for a short story of 1000 words can be just as complete and successful as one of 9000 words:

- dramatise rather than summarise important scenes
- develop background information (but beware of flashbacks)
- write additional scenes (first asking yourself if they advance the action or merely repeat what's already known)
- add characters who might take the story in new and profitable directions
- expand upon appropriate aspects of the setting
- add or expand upon dialogue
- give your characters a richer internal life
- give more detailed descriptions of the characters
- relax the style if it's too clipped (unless a clipped style is appropriate to the tone and meaning of the story)
- be less elliptical and more discursive and generous, taking time over scenes, emotions and incidents.

ORGANISATION IN A SHORT-STORY COLLECTION

If you've written and published a number of short stories and wish to collect them in book form, it's important to give some thought to how they should be organised (note that the correct term is 'collection': an 'anthology' is an editor's compilation, in one volume, of the works of several writers). First, do you have enough stories for a book? Most publishers would prefer collections of 30000 words or more. More importantly, do you have sufficient stories of publishable quality? Many writers simply lump all of their stories together, without thought to theme, style or quality. Next give some thought to their unifying characteristics. It may be that your stories are simply quite diverse, or unified by voice, style, settings, themes and subject matters. Unity is unmistakeable in Anson Cameron's *Nice Shootin', Cowboy*, for example, and in E. Annie Proulx's *Close Range*. Finally, arrange the strongest or 'best' stories at the start and end of the collection, with the others arranged thematically by subject matter or to set up tensions or contrasts with those that precede and follow them; for example, a buoyant story about love could sit with a distressing one.

twelve

WRITING A NOVEL

Make them laugh, make them cry, make them wait.
CHARLES DICKENS

Where the short-story writer aims to be precise and economical, pursuing one area of complexity and setting up simple and incisive oppositions, the novelist can afford to be more relaxed, expansive and discursive. Writing the short story should not be seen as a proving ground for writing the novel, however, and nor should novels be seen as the greater challenge simply because they're longer than short stories. In the interests of writing the best thing they're capable of writing, experienced fiction writers may find themselves spending six weeks on one novel and six years on another, or one week on one short story and one year on another.

THE NOVEL IN THE MARKETPLACE

literary and popular

Fiction is often divided, for convenience, into two categories: literary and popular. Literary fiction is sometimes thought of as highbrow, difficult, and concerned with fine writing and weighty ideas and issues, and popular fiction as slight, clumsily written and forgettable.

Not only is such a division arbitrary, each category is misunderstood. Patrick White's powerful literary novels might deal with important ideas, but they are also funny and moving, while John Le Carré's spy novels, Elmore Leonard's crime thrillers and Georgette Heyer's historical romances are complex, intelligent and well-written. There is also a middle range of fiction: carefully crafted novels that deal with important contemporary issues and yet reach a large general audience; for instance, books by Margaret Drabble, John Irving, Joanna Trollope and Anne Tyler.

There are several types of literary novels. Some, like Joseph Heller's *Catch-22*, explore a theme; Kate Grenville's *Lilian's Story* is a study of character; James Frazier's *Cold Mountain* tells a story; Italo Calvino's *If on a Winter's Night a Traveller* is postmodern in its exploration of the creative act itself. These are not clear-cut categories, of course: in E. L. Doctorow's *Billy Bathgate*, theme, portrait and story come together.

genre novels

There are many genres of popular fiction, including romance, adventure, war, spy, crime, erotic, historical, western, science fiction, and 'sex-and-shopping', as well as sub-genres, such as the crime-novel categories 'psychological mystery', 'police procedural' and 'private eye'. The techniques of plotting, characterisation, setting, dialogue and point of view apply equally to these as to fiction considered more 'serious' or 'literary'.

Certain conventions govern each genre, and aficionados

usually enjoy a certain predictability in form, structure, style and hero type, but fashions also change, and the best writers, such as the mystery writer Ruth Rendell, strive to extend conventions and forge new ones.

CHILDREN'S NOVELS

Children of primary-school age move from picture books to little 'chapter' novels, which may be fewer than 5000 words long with line drawings throughout, and from these to longer novels with fewer—or no—illustrations. Children's reading abilities and tastes vary dramatically, however, so that one ten-year-old might develop a taste for 70 000-word fantasy novels and another struggle with a 10 000-word chapter book. There is also a relatively new category, the Young Adult novel, of 35 000 words and up, for older teenagers. Some, like Melina Marchetta's *Looking for Alibrandi*, Maureen McCarthy's *Queen Kat, Carmel and St. Jude Get a Life*, and my own *The Divine Wind*, have later been successfully republished as 'cross-over' novels aimed at a general adult readership.

Children of primary-school age like to read about children slightly older than themselves who solve problems and achieve a degree of competence. Popular subjects are adventure, school life, quests and 'goodies' triumphing over 'baddies'. These children prefer a direct writing style, strong imagery and clearly defined characters, and may be bored by long passages of dialogue, long descriptions, slow beginnings, a 'twee' approach or a moralising tone.

Teenage boys like to read about humorous subjects, war,

space travel, adventure, and technological and sword-and-sorcery fantasy. Teenage girls' tastes tend to be more sophisticated: they may like mystery and adventure novels, but will also appreciate novels about relationships, moral issues, love and personal identity. Many writers for young adults deal with sensitive contemporary matters such as family break-ups, drugs, youth suicide and teenage sexuality, with the result that Young Adult fiction has become the subject of considerable debate. Some adults have argued that it's too bleak and should offer hope; others argue that it's realistic and its readers resilient, thankful to be informed and able to exercise choice.

Children's fiction is generally overlooked and undervalued by adult literary commentators, but it's amongst the most interesting fiction being published. Also, the environment created by parents, teachers, booksellers, other children's writers and the children themselves is generous and supportive, and most novels for children sell in much greater quantities than most novels for adults. This doesn't mean that writing for children is quick and easy, however. It demands time, care, sympathy, skill and familiarity with the world of children's fiction. Don't 'write down' to children, treat them as different beings or confuse simplicity with simplemindedness.

HOW LONG SHOULD A NOVEL BE?

As with the short story, the novel may be classified in terms of length. There are many terms applied to shorter works: the little 20 000-word westerns available in newsagents and supermarkets are often called 'novelettes'; Tobias Wolff's *The Barracks Thief*, and Helen Garner's *The Children's Bach*, at 27 000 words and 30 000 words respectively, may be called novellas; and Liam Davison's *The White Woman*, at about 47 000 words, is a short novel. A novel is generally understood to be about 50 000 words and upwards.

Short novels tend to have few characters, limited settings, a fairly contained situation and cover a relatively small canvas. When asked what differences he noted between writing his short stories and writing *The Cement Garden*, his 47 000-word first novel, Ian McEwan replied:

> I was fairly confident because I knew that my material, even when pared down, as it was, could only take the shape of a novel. There are certain strengths of the short story form which I tried to build into the novel. I wanted it to be a short novel, a novel you could read in one go. I wanted it to hold the reader's attention for two or three hours in the way that a short story writer would expect to hold the reader's attention for half an hour or forty minutes. I quite deliberately chose a fairly closed off situation, partly out of a sense of nervousness about having to deal with too much too soon all at once. There's a limited number of characters and the drama ends when the outside world intervenes.

Longer novels tend to be more ambitious and promise different rewards. I enjoyed Charles Frazier's 170 000-word American Civil War novel, *Cold Mountain*, for example, for its leisurely but relevant digressions, richly drawn characters, variety of settings, arcane knowledge, tension and suspense. Owing to its density and richness, *Cold Mountain* feels complex, but the question at the heart of it is very simple: Will the army deserter, Inman, succeed in making his way home to be with Ada, the woman he loves?

As an exercise read the short story in the previous chapter as though it were the beginning of a novel and map out the rest of the plot.

HOW CHAPTERS WORK

Most novels are constructed of stages which may be termed chapters, even if they're not named or numbered as such. Chapters, like scenes, act like building blocks, of little use alone but vital when joined to others. Remember that chapters should advance the story and have a degree of cohesion, so when planning each one try to consider the following questions: What is going to happen? Why? Where? Who is involved? What is said? How will it begin? End? What has happened before this? What's going to happen next?

The first chapter is vital, and most writers use it to establish the main character, central issue (often the main character just before or in the midst of a crisis), time and setting, and convey a sense of the tone (for example, rollicking, sad, ironical). If these elements are missing, readers may flounder and decide not to read on.

The chapters in the main body of the text will then build on the first chapter. For example, they might introduce new characters (if there are several major characters then it's best to introduce them gradually, over several chapters), change the apparent plot direction and reverse the characters' fortunes.

A basic but effective device for generating suspense and encouraging readers to read on is to end chapters on a point of unresolved tension, such as a question posed, a reversal, a decision to be made or a confrontation with another character. The reader, seeking a resolution, will turn the page to find out what happens next. The follow-up, at the beginning of the next chapter (or at the beginning of a later chapter in the case of novels that take up, and then leave dangling, the affairs of more than one character) may tighten the screws further, or partly or wholly relieve the tension.

To take a simple example: Your main character is home alone waiting for her husband to return. She hears a knock on the front door and opens it to two sombre-faced policemen, one of whom says, 'I'm afraid we have some bad news.' If you stop the chapter there, the reader, along with the main character, is eager to learn what has happened and what will happen next. If you answer these questions there rather than later, then the tension is relieved too quickly, and the following chapter will feel anticlimactic.

WHY READ ON?

One of the greatest challenges for the novelist is *sustaining the narrative*. Your chapters might provide intervening peaks and lulls of tension, but how can you create a concomitant sense of tension rising *throughout* the novel? And how can you keep your readers involved at an immediate level yet also feeling that they're in good hands overall? It's a balancing act; readers want both immediate gratification and to know that you have the big picture under control.

First, it helps if a novel poses a question. We want to know, as we read Michael Ondaatje's *The English Patient*, who is the Englishman and what is his story? If this were answered too early, or the answer were trite, unbelievable or unrelated to the question, then the novel would have failed. The question posed need not be as clearcut as in *The English Patient*: portrait novels invite you to ask what *manner of person* the main character is; others invite you to engage with ideas, know a place, absorb an atmosphere, negotiate a stylistic labyrinth or play an elaborate game.

It's clear from the above that once a puzzle or sense of mystery has been established, it should not only be maintained throughout but also rise in intensity. This can be done by using some of the simple devices discussed in Chapter 9: delaying tactics, withholding information, red herrings and reversing the fortunes of the main character. And it all needs to be done without the readers feeling it is contrived.

If you are dealing with several characters, then leaving one high and dry in order to take up the story of another for a while will naturally create suspense. Novelists like Thomas Keneally know how to place diverse characters in exotic or interesting settings and situations, so that the energy created by their varying relationships with one another achieves narrative momentum.

It also helps to vary the pace, a reflective chapter to follow an active one, for example, or chapters alternating between various characters at different stages of the story. Most novels contain sub-plots which, while related to the heart of the novel, may add meaning, alter the pace and act as complications for the main character.

At some point readers will want to identify and understand the element of causality that drives the novel. This may be apparent from the start—for example, Inman's need, in *Cold Mountain*, to escape the horrors of the Civil War and be reunited with the woman he loves—or revealed at the end, as in the case of a detective uncovering the identity of a murderer in a mystery novel. A novel may also conceal secrets of various kinds, but these should not be telegraphed too obviously or too early.

Turning points act as 'hooks' to the reader, and while often dramatic and related to plot, they need not be. A shift of tone—for example, from mellow to agitated—can mark a turning point.

LET THE READER DWELL

I have been discussing the importance of forward momentum in novel writing but readers also like to dwell for a while with a character, place, idea or atmosphere, or simply with the language itself. We urge Inman on as he traverses the treacherous landscape of *Cold Mountain*, but also relish his various sojourns along the way. We're absorbed by the building of a bridge in Michael Ondaatje's *In the Skin of a Lion*, some corners of European history in Louis de Bernières's *Captain Corelli's Mandolin*, and photography in Delia Falconer's *The Service of Clouds*.

A CONVENTIONAL STRUCTURE FOR YOUR FIRST NOVEL

Here is a conventional but workable approach to structuring a first novel. Treat it as a starting point only, or to get you out of trouble, for experience, ambition and wide reading will soon reveal the many alternative approaches available.

Conceive of your novel as four equal parts of fifty to sixty pages each. The first part sets up the characters and situation and poses a problem, question or conflict that gets the story going. Part 2 shows the characters beginning to move as a result, but ends with further complications for them (for example, making incorrect decisions, deciding late, or failing to act). In part 3 the characters continue to work through the issues, perhaps shifting alliances, correcting errors, having partial successes—though things might also get worse for them. Part 4 shows the problem being solved, or failing to be solved, and the consequences of that.

thirteen

THE WORDS ON THE PAGE

If I am not clear, the world around me collapses.
STENDAHL

Absorbing characters and exciting plots alone won't compel readers. The words on the page—the style—must also compel. The story or novel we 'dream' is always perfect and shimmering; then we start to write and the words never match the dream. Our job as writers is to narrow the gap. When asked why he rewrote the last page of *A Farewell to Arms* thirty-nine times, Ernest Hemingway said that he was 'getting the words right'. Henry Green took nine years to write *Party Going*, James Joyce a week to get the correct order of words in a short sentence, Gustave Flaubert days to find an appropriate adjective. When the novelist and short-story writer Gerald Murnane was asked what he wrote, he answered, 'Sentences', and V. S. Naipaul aims to write 'plain, concrete statements, adding meaning to meaning in simple stages'. In the previous chapters I mention structural techniques for holding readers' attention, including partial disclosures, turning points and red herrings, but you should be holding the reader long before this—through effective words and the effective arrangement of words. It may be necessary for you to 'unlearn' the desire to write a perfect, polished manuscript in the first draft and recognise that writing fiction often means moving from the roughly hewn to the refined in a series of drafts.

ORDER OUT OF CHAOS

As beginner writers, we know that *we* are messy scavengers; it doesn't seem credible that *real* writers are. But, as the previous chapters show, the stories and novels that we love to read, that seem so seamless, unified and immutable, probably started as makeshift assemblages of random ideas, thoughts and memories, tempered by mischance, waste, inconsistency, indecision and serendipitous luck. Even then the characters that absorb us and the plots that grip us are merely patterns of words and sentences, tied to the emotional habits and impulses of the author; add to, subtract from or alter the words and sentences and you'd have a different story or novel.

If you're progressing in fits and starts, take heart—here's Amy Tan on writing her second novel, *The Kitchen God's Wife*:

> I [told] myself that no matter how bad the story was, I should simply go on like a rat in a maze, turning the corner when I arrived at it.
>
> And so I started to write another story, about a woman who was cleaning a house, the messy house I thought I should be cleaning. After 30 pages, the house was tidy, and I had found a character I liked. I abandoned all the pages about

the tidy house. I wrote and rewrote six times another 30 pages, and found a question in her heart. I abandoned the pages and kept the question and put that in my heart. I wrote and rewrote 150 pages and then I found myself at a crisis point. The woman had turned sour on me. Her story sounded to me like one long complaint...

Who knows where inspiration comes from? Perhaps it arises from desperation. Whatever the case, one day I found myself asking, 'But *why* is she telling this story?' And she answered back: 'Of course I'm crabby! I'm talking, talking, talking, no one to talk to. Who's listening?' And I realised: A story should be a gift. She needs to *give* her story to someone...So what I have written, finally, is a story told by a mother to her daughter...

I wish I could say that was the end of writing my second book...But no...I still had hundreds of moments of self-doubt. I deleted hundreds of pages...

BEG, BORROW OR STEAL?

Writing is communication and so it's better to use words to express, not impress. But some writers are stylistically elegant and elaborate, and others bare and clipped—and they both communicate. Can we learn about style from another writer?

Most writers develop rather than learn a style, and it takes time and practice. Meanwhile I believe that it can benefit new writers to study the styles of writers they admire, and the best way to do that is to type out long passages of admired writing. Take note of the length, structure and patterning of the sentences, the placement of punctuation marks, word choice, and the sounds and rhythms of words and sentences, and then write your own version with your own characters and situations.

But style comes from an author's personality, too. You might admire the narrative fury, hectic energy, moral ambiguity and staccato delivery of James Ellroy's crime fiction, but is it *you*?

And style is determined by the material. Ultimately you have to be clear about the story or novel that's possessing you, and find the correct form for it—not the one that's taught or copied but the one that feels true to you. A borrowed style won't always sound fresh and original, and regular borrowing may ultimately bury your natural style. Let another writer's style teach you something that you can then discard or rework until you have your own.

WORDS

Writers work with words. Words have sounds, associations, suggestive power, rhythm, fixed and slippery meanings as well as concrete and abstract qualities. The English language is a living language and so it changes constantly: new words are invented and old ones are used in new ways. Yet although change is inevitable and irresistible, it pays writers to be clear, efficient and precise, irrespective of the subject matter or audience. Most practising writers own dictionaries for the meanings of words, a thesaurus for the most appropriate word, and manuals of style and English usage.

Even profound ideas and complex issues can be conveyed using a simple, unadorned prose style. Unfamiliar words, jargon, imprecisions, unnecessary rhetorical flourishes, complicated or awkward sentence constructions and excess verbiage: these can be the enemies of clear writing. They may deceive, limit the reader's ability to understand, lead to ambiguity or act as a cloak for writers who don't have a clear grasp of their material. As Gustave Flaubert said:

> Whatever the thing you wish to say, there is but one noun to express it, but one verb to give it movement, but one adjective to qualify it; you must seek until you find this noun, this verb, this adjective.

choose the best word

Here are some general guidelines for choosing the best word. It all depends on the circumstances, of course; for example, your characters won't always choose the best word when they *speak*.

- Use an everyday English word in preference to a foreign phrase, a scientific word or jargon; e.g. 'procedure' for *modus operandi,* 'underwater' for 'subaqueous', 'quit' for 'exit the situation'.
- Choose shorter or more common words over longer or rarely-used words; e.g. 'variety' instead of 'multiformity'.
- Use a simple verb in place of a fancy one; e.g. 'start' instead of 'commence'.
- Avoid clichés and words and phrases that have become meaningless through overuse and misuse; e.g. 'fabulous', 'raging desire', 'colourful personality', 'in the final analysis', 'gorgeous', 'level playing field'.
- Avoid euphemisms—expressions whose purpose is concealment or protecting the sensibilities of readers;

e.g. 'manhood' for 'penis', 'downsizing' for 'sacking' and 'comfort station' for 'toilet' or 'lavatory'.

- Check for ambiguous meanings, as with the word 'sweet' in this example: The sweet salesgirl walked him to the door.
- Choose specific, clear and concrete words over general, vague and abstract ones. Notice the weak specification of the sentences in A compared with those in B:

  A The girl had lunch in the park. (Which girl? What did she eat? Where in the park?)

  The picnic was ruined by unfavourable weather. (Sleet? Hail? Rain?)

  B Jeannie sat under a gum tree and ate a ham sandwich.

  The picnic was ruined by rain.

- Use a dictionary whenever you're unsure of a word's meaning or spelling. I recently assessed a manuscript in which the author wrote 'disinterested' instead of 'uninterested' and 'gambolling' instead of 'gambling'.
- Use a thesaurus. Imagine that you want to use a verb similar to 'examine', but 'examine' doesn't have quite the meaning you want. A thesaurus will yield words like 'inspect', 'investigate' and 'review', together with cross-references to related meanings, such as 'inquiry', and words opposite in meaning, such as 'neglect'. Use the thesaurus for the most appropriate word, however, not a clever, obscure or impressive one.
- Although it's become common practice in business and professional writing, avoid converting nouns into verbs; e.g. 'His fist *impacted* with a thud on Leftie's jaw'.
- Use simple verbs in place of verb phrases; e.g. 'spoilt' instead of 'rendered inoperable'.

- Where appropriate, appeal to the senses of touch, taste, sight, hearing and smell. In the sentence, 'He sat on a pitted rock', the reader can see and feel the rock's surface, and so is engaged and brought closer to the action.

rules for newspaper writers

Here, for your amusement, are the rules for newspaper writers from the *Bulletin* of the Minnesota Newspaper Association.

- Don't use no double negative.
- Make each pronoun agree with their antecedent.
- Join clauses good, like a conjunction should.
- About them sentence fragments.
- When dangling, watch your participles.
- Verbs has to agree with their subjects.
- Just between you and I, case is important too.
- Don't write run-on sentences they are hard to read.
- Don't use commas, which aren't necessary.
- Try to not ever split infinitives.
- Its important to use your apostrophe's correctly.
- Proofread your writing to see if you any words out.
- Correct spelling is absoluteley essential.

adjectives and adverbs

Adjectives (tall, white, straggly) describe nouns (man, wall, tree), while adverbs (quickly, awkwardly, stupidly) describe verbs (ran, jumped, spoke). If a noun or a verb is strong, however, there may be no need to describe it; '*carcass* of a dog' could stand for 'dead body of a dog' for example, and '*glided* across the room' could stand for 'moved slowly and gracefully across the room'. When adjectives and adverbs seem necessary they should be lively and well-chosen; for example, 'cheerlessly' might be better than 'unhappily', and 'flimsy' better than 'thin'. Although I admit to an occasional fondness for a string of vivid adjectives when circumstances demand it ('She was tall, hectic, tensely boned...'), I think it's generally better to use them sparingly. 'An old swagman lounged in the shade of a gum tree' is preferable to 'A shabby, unshaven old man of about seventy sat like a discarded scarecrow in the shade of an untidy, bark-stripped eucalyptus tree'.

How concrete or specific should you be? It depends upon your intention at any point. If a character is running because he's being chased, then he, and the reader, will be content to know that he's running through 'autumn' leaves; if he's jogging, and appreciating his surroundings, then he'll notice that the leaves are 'brown', 'dry' and 'crackling under his feet'.

SENTENCES

Varying the pace, length and construction of sentences will help to enliven prose style. A succession of long, rolling, sing-song sentences may lull readers, and the impact of the passage be lost. Where appropriate, use short sentences, for example, to establish a mood of tension and anxiety in a description of fear or a fight. Longer, slower, more complex sentences can convey an atmosphere of contemplation and peacefulness, or regret and sadness—but if they're too long they may run the risk of grammatical errors or different ideas competing for emphasis. If a long sentence proves troublesome, shorten it or restructure it as two or more briefer sentences.

Think also about the arrangement of the parts of the sentence, asking yourself where the emphasis should lie. Note the shifts of emphasis in these sentences:

A great sadness settled in him when Jeannie died, and he refused to leave the house.

When Jeannie died a great sadness settled in him and he refused to leave the house.

He refused to leave the house because a great sadness had settled in him when Jeannie died.

sentence economy and accuracy

In the following examples, sentences A and B are similar in meaning, but B is more concise. Unless you have a particular reason for choosing the longer construction (for example, the narrator or characters write or speak like that), aim for conciseness.

- *avoid afterthoughts*

  A A porch had been added to the house, and a carport as well.

  B A porch and a carport had been added to the house.

- *avoid 'the fact that'*

  A Bill was aware of the fact that many people were homeless.

  B Bill was aware that many people were homeless.

- *avoid redundancies*

  A Nita was praised for her hard work and commended for her loyalty.

  B Nita was praised for her hard work and loyalty.

- *avoid tautologies (saying the same thing twice)*
  A Each individual case will be examined on its own merits.
  B Each case will be examined on its merits.

- *avoid unnecessary use of 'that', 'which' and 'who'*
  A The facts that are given in this report are disturbing.
  He was found in a park which is on the river.
  His friend, who was a nurse, stopped the bleeding.
  B The facts in this report are disturbing.
  He was found in a park on the river.
  His friend, a nurse, stopped the bleeding.

- *avoid the passive voice*
  A The car stolen by Mark was a Porsche.
  B Mark stole a Porsche.

- *avoid 'manner', 'nature' and 'character'*
  A She responded in an angry manner to the accusation.
  B She responded angrily to the accusation.

- *avoid unnecessary qualifiers*
  A The rail strike made it rather difficult for me to get to work.
  B The rail strike made it difficult for me to get to work.

- *use verbs in place of noun constructions*
  A Margot's pep talks brought about a reduction in bickering.
  B Margot's pep talks reduced bickering.

- *replace a phrase with a word*
  A His new car had the capacity to carry several people.
  B His new car could carry several people.

- *express negatives as positives*
  A He was not relaxed about the operation.
  B He was anxious about the operation.

- *avoid using 'case' and 'instance'*
  A In many cases burglaries had not been reported.
  B Many burglaries had not been reported.
- *avoid unnecessary repetition*
  A He stirred in quantities of cement, of powder and of sand.
  B He stirred in quantities of cement, powder and sand.
- *avoid roundabout constructions and repetitions*
  A The reason why the Department rejected Sergeant Challis's promotion was due to the fact that he did not file his reports on time, a factor which could have been avoided if he'd taken the trouble to pay attention to details.
  B The Department rejected Challis's promotion because he didn't file his reports on time.

PARAGRAPHS

Paragraphs comprise one or more sentences that develop or explore an idea or action. An effective paragraph is like a composition, with a beginning, middle and end. Generally the first sentence announces the topic of the paragraph, the following sentences, arranged logically, elaborate upon it, and the final sentence rounds off the sense of the paragraph. In itself a paragraph can also announce a topic to be explored more fully in the following paragraphs, summarise or conclude a topic already explored, or act as a transition from one paragraph idea to another.

Where an idea or action requires more than one paragraph for development, each paragraph should deal with a separate stage of it. Where there is a new idea or action, start a new paragraph.

Try to vary the length and pace of paragraphs, according to your intention at that point; a series of short paragraphs will help convey speed and tension in a car chase, for example. Avoid a succession of one-sentence paragraphs as used in newspapers, and beware of competing ideas and clutter in very long paragraphs.

TENSES

Many beginner writers change tenses without being aware of it. The tense of a story or novel should be consistent unless you have a good technical or creative reason for changing it. Most writing is in the past tense ('Martin cut a hole in the fence and escaped'). The present tense ('Martin cuts a hole in the fence and escapes') is also popular, for it encourages immediacy and dramatic tension. Its effectiveness is strikingly illustrated in these collections of short stories: Margaret Atwood's *Bluebeard's Egg*, Bobbie Ann Mason's *Shiloh and Other Stories* and Anson Cameron's *Nice Shootin', Cowboy*. However, using the present tense can be inflexible, sound jerky, and raise questions of logic about narrative stance on actions that may be continuous, habitual or discrete. Fiction is never written exclusively in the future tense ('Martin will cut a hole in the fence and escape') but may consist of brief passages— often toward the end of a story or novel—to project into or speculate about the future beyond the scope of the plot.

To maintain the correct tense it can be useful for new writers to identify the moment at which the narrative voice is speaking (relating what happened in the near or distant past; relating what is happening right now; relating what will happen in the future). With experience, and the desire to take risks, you may want to vary tenses to achieve certain effects; see, for example, Jennifer Johnston's *The Christmas Tree* and Michael Ondaatje's *In the Skin of a Lion*.

SYMBOLS

A symbol, in the broadest sense of the term, is anything which signifies something else. For example, a cross symbolises Christ and Christianity, and white feathers, denoting cowardice, were handed to men who did not enlist in the armed forces during the First World War. Words, too, engage in this kind of transformation: the diamond earring worn by a character in a story can become a sexual wink, a symbol of the availability of the person wearing it. Symbols are not static: they acquire meaning over a period of time. But, as Freud said, sometimes a cigar is just a cigar.

SYNTAX DETERMINES CONTENT DETERMINES SYNTAX...

What you have to say (the content) decides the words you use to say it (the form). Content usually comes before form, but the right form will illuminate the content. In this way the craft of writing is circular. As we choose the words to say what we want to say, we discover what it is we want to say.

Here is Holden, from Murray Bail's novel, *Holden's Performance*:

Holden shuffled forward several paces. A lumpen clumsiness spread from his limbs, blurring his vision and all distinctions, a moral condition—a know-nothingness—which he would increasingly find himself struggling against.

At first sight we might say that Bail's style lacks elegance, but the words and their arrangement are in fact well chosen: syntax is psychology here. The hesitations and awkwardness are deliberate, intended to mirror Holden's physical and moral condition. The style reflects the character and the character is reflected in the style. Katherine Mansfield said, of writing her short story, 'Miss Brill':

> In 'Miss Brill' I chose not only the length of each sentence, but even the sound of every sentence. I chose the rise and fall of every paragraph to fit her, and to fit her on that day of that very moment. After I'd written it I read it aloud—numbers of times—just as one would *play over* a musical composition—trying to get it nearer and nearer to the expression of Miss Brill—until it fitted her.

Syntactical arrangements can reflect moods, settings and actions, too. Here is the opening paragraph of Ernest Hemingway's 1929 novel, *A Farewell to Arms*, followed by an analysis of it by Joan Didion, an American novelist and critic:

> In the late summer of that year we lived in a house in a village that looked across from the river and the plain to the mountains. In the bed of the river there were pebbles and boulders, dry and white in the sun, and the water was clear and swiftly moving and blue in the channels. Troops went by the house and down the road and the dust they raised powdered the leaves of the trees. The trunks of the trees too

were dusty and the leaves fell early that year and we saw the troops marching along the road and the dust rising and leaves, stirred by the breeze, falling and the soldiers marching and afterward the road bare and white except for the leaves.

Joan Didion wrote:

That paragraph…bears examination: four deceptively simple sentences, one hundred and twenty-six words, the arrangement of which remains as mysterious and thrilling to me now as it did when I first read them, at twelve or thirteen, and imagined that if I studied them closely enough and practised hard enough I might one day arrange one hundred and twenty-six words myself. Only one of the words has three syllables. Twenty-two have two. The other hundred and three have one. Twenty-four of the words are 'the', fifteen are 'and'. There are four commas. The liturgical cadence of the paragraph derives in part from the placement of the commas (their presence in the second and fourth sentences, their absence in the first and third), but also from the repetition of 'the' and 'and', creating a rhythm so pronounced that the omission of 'the' before the word 'leaves' in the fourth sentence ('and we saw the troops marching along the road and the dust rising and leaves, stirred by the breeze, falling') casts exactly what it was meant to cast, a chill, a premonition, a foreshadowing of the story to come, the awareness that the author has already shifted his attention from late summer to a darker season. The power of the paragraph, offering as it does the illusion but not the fact of specificity, derives precisely from this kind of deliberate omission, from the tension of withheld information. In the late summer of *what* year? *What* river, *what* mountains, *what* troops?

Didion's analysis also shows that rules can be broken. Hemingway's repetitions are deliberate—but they're also successful, for he had a masterly grasp of the techniques of writing and knew when and how to break the rules to achieve a desired effect.

As an exercise, consider this image: A woman alights from a train. She's elderly, and nervous about the pension money in her purse; *or*, she's young and on her way to the gym. She's been to the hospital to see her dying father, possibly for the last time; *or*, she's about to embrace her lover, who is waiting for her there on the platform. Visualise each situation, then attempt to convey the setting and the woman's inner and outer states in each case, paying attention to the psychological, syntactic and symbolic harmonies of your prose.

TONE

In addition to creating 'word pictures', prose styles carry a tone; for example, *ironic*. Irony involves incongruity and the tension between opposites; it may be conveyed through events and outcomes (an abusive husband and father being voted Family Man of the Year), or stylistically (by describing terrible events in a calm voice). A *suggestive* tone hints at meaning, encouraging the reader to read between the lines, sometimes mistakenly. *Foreshadowing* gives clues to outcomes. Shirley Jackson's famous short story, 'The Lottery' uses irony, suggestiveness and foreshadowing to powerful effect. A suspenseful tone is achieved when readers start to ask questions which they hope (or even fear) will be answered. There is immediacy in a direct, forthright style. Sometimes tone can achieve a distancing effect through scepticism, satire and comic irony, as though the author is unimpressed, unmoved or frankly scornful.

opening tone

The art of starting a story or novel is often the art of finding the tone, and so tone may waver in the drafting stages. By the time a work of fiction is ready for submission, however, the tone should be firmly established and apparent to the reader in the opening sentences and paragraphs. Here are the opening few lines of Alice Munro's short story, 'Miles City, Montana':

My father came across the field carrying the body of the boy who had drowned. There were several men together, returning from the search, but he was the one carrying the body. The men were muddy and exhausted, and walked with their heads down, as if they were ashamed. Even the dogs were dispirited, dripping from the cold river. When they all set out, hours before, the dogs were nervy and yelping, the men tense and determined, and there was a constrained, unspeakable excitement about the whole scene. It was understood that they might find something horrible.

The boy's name was Steve Gauley. He was eight years old. His hair and clothes were mud-coloured now and carried some bits of dead leaves, twigs, and grass. He was like a heap of refuse that had been left out all winter. His face was turned in to my father's chest, but I could see a nostril, an ear, plugged with greenish mud.

I don't think so. I don't think I really saw all this. Perhaps I saw my father carrying him, and other men following along, and the dogs, but I would not have been allowed close enough to see something like mud in his nostril. I must have heard someone talking about that and imagined that I saw it. I see his face unaltered except for the mud—Steve Gauley's familiar, sharp-honed, sneaky-looking face—and it wouldn't have been like that; it would have been bloated and changed and perhaps muddied all over after so many hours in the water.

The tone is careful and precise, giving a strong sense of the narrator, the place, the situation and the atmosphere, and even hinting at the narrator's ambiguous feelings toward the dead boy. We start in the midst of dramatic events; there's no unnecessary build-up. The pace is suitably unhurried, in keeping with the tenor of the events and the act of remembering, with short sentences announcing each new stage of meaning, and longer ones elaborating upon them. The narrative stance is clearly established—looking back in time—but then there's that arresting third paragraph, throwing doubt on what has gone before it and informing us that one of the themes of the story is the hazards and tricks of memory.

'Caress the detail', Nabokov said; 'every detail is an omen and a cause', according to Jorge Luis Borges. In the above extract, details, such as the dogs, the plug of mud and the boy's face, are conveyed vividly, and have long-reaching implications.

fourteen

TROUBLESHOOTING

> *I have never considered myself as a good writer. But*
> *I'm one of the world's great rewriters.*
> JAMES A. MICHENER

So, you're suffering from writer's block, or your manuscript has been rejected several times, or you sense there's something wrong with it...

Inexperienced writers often feel that revision is failure, believing that experienced writers sit down and write perfect first drafts. In fact, editing and rewriting are essential parts of the process of writing, and this chapter is intended to help you identify possible faults in your manuscripts. It's a distillation of observations and lessons learned the hard way from my years as a novelist and short-story writer, writing teacher, competition judge and manuscript assessor.

WRITER'S BLOCK

All writers are 'blocked' from time to time. The reasons for it include a failure of nerve, domestic and personal upheavals, fear of rejection, boredom, insufficient preparation and miscalculating the scope of an idea. These last two reasons are probably the most common; certainly they account for why I'd been forced to abandon four novels over the years.

What to do about it? First, ask honestly of yourself why you stopped writing. Perhaps the project was beyond your writing capabilities, you were bored with it, or the emotional and physical stress was too harmful. Why persevere? Start a new, more absorbing or manageable project.

Perhaps you haven't prepared sufficiently. Put the manuscript aside and think more about it, carry out further research or write 'around' the topic until you find answers or a path out. If these don't work start a new project; it could be that weeks, months, even years later you'll find the solution you need, either subconsciously or through luck, greater wisdom or a certain 'trigger', such as a complementary idea. Patience, and better preparation, enabled me to complete two of the novels I'd abandoned.

In the case of the other two I was 'blocked' because they lacked the substance to become novels, but I was able to rework them successfully as short stories. There are other types of miscalculation too; for example, you might have too much material so that your story or novel is unnecessarily cluttered or complex.

Perhaps you're on the right path and can see your destination ahead of you but have encountered an obstacle, such as not knowing how your main character came by a vital piece of information at a crucial point in the story. If thinking and writing your way through it is too difficult or making you lose heart (although a long walk can work wonders), try simply spiriting yourself to the other side of that obstacle—just go on as if you'd solved the problem. It may be that when you look back you can see where and how you should have proceeded.

Or take Raymond Chandler's advice and *make* something happen. He once said that whenever he wrote himself into a corner he'd get the story going again by having a man walk through the door wielding a gun. Of course this only works if the action is logical, inevitable or accountable rather than merely grafted on because all else has failed.

MAIN PROBLEM AREAS

What should you do when you're not blocked but sense weaknesses in the manuscript or it keeps getting rejected? Here are the main problem areas of novels and short stories.

the subject itself

New—and experienced—writers often write too much owing to a lack of focus (Sara Paretsky threw out three hundred pages of her novel, *Tunnel Vision*, saying: 'I was kind of meandering and it just didn't have a shape') or burden themselves with complex, complicated or competing ideas. It may be necessary to simplify the theme and coolly cut inessential ideas, characters, incidents and sub-plots.

The subject might also suffer from:

- your lack of engagement with it (i.e. it's not been one that you've badly wanted to write but one that's merely fashionable)
- too much exposition and instruction at the expense of characters and story (this is often a problem with historical and science-fiction works)

- inauthenticity, anachronisms or shallowness owing to a lack of research
- being insignificant, or falsely significant
- holding no intrinsic interest for most readers, or not being interesting *yet* (see the novel *Perfume*, by Patrick Süskind, for a clever, stylish account of the manufacture of scent in eighteenth-century France, an otherwise 'specialist' subject matter)
- ideas and feelings that are false, borrowed, unexamined or dishonest
- narrowness of range, so that there's little awareness of the wider world or other ramifications
- secondary concerns (sub-plots, minor characters) overwhelming the main concerns
- an over-reliance on the plan, at the expense of instincts or commonsense
- a too awkward meshing of two or more conventions (e.g. a crime novel with a gay 'coming out' novel)
- no sense of a goal or end-point in the plot or the lives of the characters; nothing driving the story, in other words
- being too close to you, or too autobiographical (learn to stand apart from the material so that you can meddle with it creatively)
- being too ambitious for the marketplace; i.e. you've written a trilogy of full-length, closely intertwined novels and assumed that a publisher will take the whole thing on.

the characters

Apart from characters who fail to elicit interest, sympathy or empathy in the reader, the most common weakness is characters who are full of interesting personality traits but simply don't do anything; that is, never make mistakes, take charge of situations, act on their desires or attempt to change or preserve the status quo. As Chapter 4 shows, character is action and action is character. It helps if something is at stake for characters in fiction, such as a job, a lover, a reputation, or if there is a sense of urgency regarding impending or conflicting deadlines.

Other problems with character include:

- personalities that are too one-dimensional
- characters swamped by the demands of a busy plot
- too many characters
- too few characters (if you're working with a pair of characters who fail to budge or engage with each other, the addition of a third, intervening character can introduce tension or new plot directions)
- the wrong character is filtering the story to the reader
- the characters carry *your* ideological attitudes and prejudices rather than their own
- the characters are too shallow, or too black-and-white (even a murderer might love his mum), or mere puppets of the author
- the motives driving the characters are unconvincing, inconsistent, convoluted or barely credible
- demands of the plot are forcing the characters to act out of character
- the characters fail to grow, change or learn anything (unless this is your point)
- the main character faces too many obstacles or problems
- the main character faces too few obstacles or problems

- luck, coincidence or the cavalry are intervening to solve the main character's problems when the solution (certainly at the end) should be in his or her hands
- all of the characters are alike, or speak with a voice that is too similar
- minor or secondary characters are given equal weight with the major characters
- the characters are swamped by ideas or theme
- there are too many interesting but functionless characters
- the main characters too closely resemble you or your friends and so have no life of their own
- too many of the characters are clichéd (spinster librarian, plodding policeman, slow-moving farmer)
- the characters are ill-served by their dialogue (i.e. they speak too much, not enough, sound stilted, are too refined or educated for their own good)
- the characters apparently don't have lives or acquaintances and relationships beyond the immediate demands of the plot
- the characters have busy but irrelevant lives outside the demands of the plot.

emotional impact

I'd not argue that readers *must* be moved emotionally by the characters and plot of a work of fiction—after all, many novels and stories appeal because they are coolly intellectual, ironic, clever, detached, playful—but I believe that most readers *prefer* to be. See if you can gauge the emotional pitch of your story or novel. It will fail to move readers positively if the characters are unappealing to begin with, or their experiences either too overwrought or too muted.

structure

First novels are commonly misshapen owing to misjudged emphases, too short owing to under-development or missed opportunities, or too long owing to indulgence, a lack of focus or a failure to be selective.

Other problems of structure include:

- the opening is too slow (Chekhov said to 'start in the middle of things') or confusing. If the first few pages— even the first paragraph—don't 'hook' and then hold the reader, your work won't get a reading
- the opening is too confusing
- the ending is lazy, weak, inconsistent with the build-up, unlikely, or emotionally unsatisfying
- a particular storyline starts the work but is unaccountably abandoned and a different storyline taken to completion
- too much is happening
- there's an over-reliance on coincidence
- the story's too formulaic (as in the case of genre fiction) and so holds no surprises for the reader
- too many loose ends remain
- every cul-de-sac and tangent of plot and character has been explored and so the story spreads sideways without also moving forwards
- the opposite: there's a sense of forward but not sideways movement
- the surprises and twists come at the beginnings rather than the ends of chapters
- the flashbacks are too long, too frequent or appear too early.

suspense and tension

All narratives should create uncertainty. Suspense for the reader (and for the characters) is bound up with anxiety about the characters' choices and their outcomes. The following factors may weaken suspense:

- characters who have nothing at stake
- no sense of a direction, outcome or goal in the story
- no time imperative for the characters and so no sense of urgency
- no doubts about the final outcome
- no partial outcomes or blunders during the story
- endings telegraphed, or telegraphed too clearly or too soon
- no anticipation; a good beginning will pose a question and hint at the probable direction, yet also be misleading
- a failure to withhold or delay information at crucial points
- no surprises, sudden reversals or hidden secrets
- too much has been left out
- not enough has been left out
- no sense of being in the dark with the main character or alternatively, of knowing things the main character doesn't know.

word pictures

Perhaps, as you work, you can 'see' the settings and the characters in your mind's eye, but to the reader they are hazily rendered, or the action is mostly internal, in the form of characters musing about things. Good writing evokes 'pictures in the head'. Use concrete nouns, vivid adjectives, reverberating similes and sensory detail to encourage your readers to taste the staleness of the coffee, smell the toxins in the air, hear the timbre in a voice, stroke a lover's face, watch the sun set.

characters and landscape

You have evoked an interesting landscape but forgotten what is *humanly* interesting about it. Cormac McCarthy's *Blood Meridian* and Murray Bail's *Eucalyptus* weave complex stories of people through landscape. If *only* about landscape or *only* about human behaviour, they would have failed as novels.

wrong point of view

Where your subject matter is raw or confronting, you might find the distancing effect of the third-person point of view more effective than the intimacy of the first-person. Alternatively, where the subject matter is quieter, the third-person point of view might lack the 'pull' and intimacy of the first-person.

You might also have chosen to tell the story through an inappropriate character. An observer might be more effective than one of the main characters, for example, or a different main character might have more vital or interesting things at stake, or the viewpoints of several characters might give much-needed density and complexity to your tale.

Viewpoint is also related to tone. An ironic tone might suit a story about complacent, grasping, self-absorbed characters, but seem jarring in a story about characters who deserve compassion.

missed opportunities

Often these are spotted by a reader or editor: the interesting but undeveloped minor character, or the sub-plot that offers more than the main plot.

But writers can train themselves to identify scenes that have been glossed-over or merely reported but deserve action and dialogue to bring them alive on the page. Learn to recognise moments of dramatic potential in your stories and novels.

problems of style

Most new writers are poor stylists. They lack an ear for the rhythms of language, make errors of grammar, spelling and punctuation (and assume wrongly that it's the editor's job to correct them), or are flowery or ornate when a plainer style would do. Other common weaknesses include:

- holding inflexible and out-of-date notions of what 'good' English is
- over-drafting and so losing the freshness of the material
- clichéd expressions
- constructing a vast superstructure of prose effects in order to impress or seem clever and forgetting the reader's need for plot and character
- sounding falsely significant and profound
- vagueness owing to an inadequate knowledge of the material.

it's all in the detail

Don't skate over essentials or linger over nonessentials, and avoid unnecessary explanations: trust your narrative and dialogue to imply and suggest. Remember that the obsessive recording of details (food, guns, forensic techniques, dress, furnishings, architecture) can bore or distract readers, yet a lack of detail can frustrate them.

learn to cut

The art of rewriting is more often than not the art of cutting. Writers learn to cut the obvious, the mundane, the unnecessary, the over-written. They ask of every character, scene, dialogue passage and description: Do I need this, or is it padding? Does it advance the story or merely repeat what is already known? Can it be shortened? Remember that superfluous material *with potential in its own right* needn't necessarily be thrown out but put aside and later reworked as a new piece.

As an exercise, take one of your short stories and either cut the beginning and the ending, or rewrite it at half or two-thirds of its original length while retaining the original intent and meaning. If the story is improved as a result, then it may be that you need to take heed of the advice, 'get in, get out, don't linger'.

who wants to read your autobiography?

You might find your experiences and beliefs interesting or compelling, but will readers? A common tendency for inexperienced fiction writers is to graft their own experiences onto their characters too transparently. Readers always seem to know when it has happened and quickly lose interest in the story.

Try viewing yourself and your experiences dispassionately before weaving them into a story. Only then can you meddle, changing outcomes or transferring experiences to invented characters.

SOME COMMON WEAKNESSES IN CRIME FICTION

In most first crime novels characterisation loses out to the demands of plot, which itself is usually too formulaic, cluttered or reliant on coincidence.

Other weaknesses include:

- detectives who don't detect but rely on luck
- unlikely but convenient oversights of the hero (e.g. failing to check the baddie for a concealed weapon)
- an over-reliance on other characters to get the hero out of trouble
- the ending is in the hands of the cavalry, not the hero
- heroes who are too brave, skilful and tough to be true, or fail to learn from their experiences (e.g. letting themselves be shot at or beaten up time after time)
- heroes who never worry about waning powers, physical prowess, growing older or moral and ethical issues
- heroes who have none of the relationships of ordinary people (e.g. with a mother, sister or friends)
- heroes who go alone to meet strangers in isolated places at the dead of night (are they out of their minds?)
- using tired old situations (would a real murderer blithely stand by and let the detective gather all the suspects together in one room and reveal his or her identity?)

- withholding obvious information from the reader
- the hero spending most of the story scratching his or her head over a niggling thought that promises to solve the mystery but always seems to evaporate
- characters who are too obviously politically correct
- Roman centurions or fifteenth-century monks holding political and social attitudes of the twenty-first century.

A JUDGE'S REPORT

I'm often asked what I'm looking for when I judge competitions for the best short-story or novel manuscript, and sometimes entrants try to second-guess me, as though believing my own written work is an indication of what I'd be looking for. Here is the report I wrote for a competition offering a prize of $5000 for the best short story:

> The organisers received a record 932 stories for the Open category. They were uneven in quality, but the best were very good and I had difficulty in deciding upon the winners and the short lists, hence the long commended and highly commended lists.
>
> What is a short story? The notion has changed over the years. In the past, stories were expected to be strongly plotted and realistic, often with a trick or clever ending. That's no longer the case. Stories these days pay more attention to character development, creating atmospheres, shifting our perceptions of a character or a situation, exploring a mood, or playing with the creative act itself—in fact, nothing much may happen in a modern story in terms of plot.

I chose about 100 stories, or a little over ten per cent, for a second reading. The remainder I rejected before completing the first page. I was looking for these sorts of qualities, not necessarily all present at once: the willingness to take risks; a touch of grace and flair in the style; an avoidance of clichéd situations and false sentimentality; the use of vivid 'word pictures'; rich characterisation; acute or quirky observations; a sense of control over the material; believable dialogue; imagined characters and situations; and finally a sense of *story*, i.e. a shift, change or movement in the narrative, or a revelation at the end, or a point made, however subtle. Ultimately, I wanted to feel that the material mattered to the author, that he or she *had* to tell this story and could not tell it in any other way.

I should stress that I did not reject stories on the grounds of subject matter but only on how the subject was handled. Nevertheless, there were too many stories that belonged to a bygone era of popular magazines, which favoured trick endings, clichéd action or romance situations; and too many anecdotes, reminiscences, philosophical treatises and other sorts of NON-fiction.

It was clear to me that many of the people who enter short story competitions never *read* short stories, or certainly not contemporary ones. Inexperienced writers should make an attempt to read the many collections and anthologies available in bookshops and libraries.

Of the 100 stories that I read twice, I weeded out those that were well-written but had little to say, started strongly and finished weakly, and were stylistically graceless.

This left me with about fifty stories that were read several times. The standard by now was pretty even, and all were publishable. With everything else being equal, I found myself being more subjective in my approach. For example, I chose stories that had an emotional impact over cold or clever ones, stories with clearly imagined characters and situations over apparently autobiographical ones, and stories with a sense of narrative movement over static, atmospheric ones, no matter how exquisitely wrought. Another judge might have applied different standards at this point.

I chose 'Remembering Argos' as the winning story. It's beautifully written, with a delicate touch and a moving tone of regret and missed opportunities.

In second place is 'The River'. It's quirky and closely focused, with stunning images and expressions, and threaded with a note of mystery and sadness.

'Isis' is the third placegetter. I was struck by the strong sense of place, the vivid characterisations, and the narrator's persona—funny/sad, perceptive and individualistic.

CONCLUSION

I hope the checklists in this chapter help you to rewrite your stories and novels. Throughout the book I have been speaking from my experience as a writer *and* reader, but don't wish to be seen as having the final say. I'm still learning. I'll never stop learning. I live with the paradoxical sense of never knowing enough about the craft of writing fiction even as I know more. I know that I'm not alone. Even as fine a stylist as Richard Ford has most of his sentences challenged by his editor, Gary Fisketjon:

He questions or comments on about eighty per cent of the sentences. And he's not proprietary about his comments, he just wants to have things to say because he thinks—and we agree—as often as I can be brought back to reconsider a sentence, the more likely I am to write a good sentence. And it's painful. It's excruciating.

It *is* painful and excruciating—but it's also an essential part of developing the craft of writing. We improve as we go along, partly by listening to expert advice but mostly by learning from our mistakes and developing the critical eye that tells us when we are not writing well. Bit by bit, we realise that we *can* improve, then that we *have* improved. We know more. We're prepared to take risks and test ourselves. And so we improve still further, and so we're rewarded.

FURTHER READING

Anderson, Don (ed.), *Contemporary Classics: the best Australian short fiction 1965–1995*, Vintage, Sydney, 1996.

Barrowman, Fergus (ed.), *The Picador Book of Contemporary New Zealand Fiction*, Picador Macmillan, London, 1996.

Bird, Carmel, *Dear Writer*, McPhee Gribble/Penguin Books, Ringwood, 1988.

Bradbury, Malcolm (ed.), *The Penguin Book of Modern British Short Stories*, Penguin Books, London, 1988.

Brande, Dorothea, *Becoming a Writer*, Macmillan, London, 1983.

Day, Marele (ed.), *How to Write Crime*, Allen & Unwin, Sydney, 1996.

Disher, Garry, *Writing Professionally*, Allen & Unwin, Sydney, 1989.

——(ed.), *Below the Waterline*, HarperCollins, Sydney, 1999.

——(ed.), *Personal Best*, HarperCollins, Sydney, 1989.

Dunn, Irina, *The Writer's Guide*, Allen & Unwin, Sydney, 1999.

Ford, Richard (ed.), *The Granta Book of the American Long Story*, Granta Books, London, 1998.

Grenville, Kate *The Writing Book*, Allen & Unwin, Sydney, 1998.

Leavitt, David and Mitchell, Mark (eds), *The Penguin Book of Gay Short Stories*, Viking, New York, 1994.

Moffett, James and McElheny, Kenneth (eds), *Points of View: An Anthology of Short Stories*, rev. edn, Mentor Penguin, New York, 1995.

Oates, Joyce Carol (ed.), *The Oxford Book of American Short Stories*, Oxford University Press, Oxford and New York, 1992.

Ondaatje, Michael (ed.), *The Faber Book of Contemporary Canadian Short Stories*, Faber and Faber, London, 1990.

Orwell, George, 'Politics and the English Language', in *Shooting an Elephant*, Harcourt, New York, 1950.

Plimpton, George (ed.), *Writers at Work: The Paris Review Interviews*, Penguin Books, London and New York (in several volumes since 1958).

Strunk, William and White, E. B., *The Elements of Style*, Macmillan, New York, 1979.

Wolff, Tobias (ed.), *The Picador Book of Contemporary American Short Stories*, Picador Macmillan, London, 1994.

SOURCES

The following is a list of sources for quotations found in this book. It aims to be scrupulous but if unsourced or incorrectly sourced quotations are identified, the author and publisher would welcome correction for future editions of the book. For permission to reproduce copyright material, we give grateful thanks.

The quotations at the head of each chapter come from Donald M. Murray, *A Writer Teaches Writing*, Houghton Mifflin, Boston, 1968, pp. 231–245 (except the quote from Virginia Woolf in Chapter 11; see 'Writing a Short Story' below).

Becoming a Writer

Carver, Raymond, 'A Storyteller's Shoptalk', in *The New York Times Book Review*, 15 February 1981, p. 18.

Rilke, Rainer Maria, from *Letters to a Young Poet*, cited in Sari Hosie, 'Writing for Writing's Sake', *Write On*, Vol. 10, No. 11, 1999, p. 7.

Theroux, Paul, 'Travels with Naipaul', *National Times*, 20 September 1985, p. 28.

O'Brien, Edna, 'Caught Between Writing and Life', *The Age*, 4 September 1982, p. 14.

Frost, Robert, in Donald M. Murray, op. cit., p. 237.

Ondaatje, Michael, in Mick Brown, 'A Devil for the Details', *Sydney Morning Herald* (Good Weekend), 3 June 2000, p. 50.

Nabokov, Vladimir, in Donald M. Murray, op. cit., p. 242.

O'Connor, Flannery, as quoted in Meg Walker, 'Can Writing be Taught?', *Palo Alto Weekly*, 6 December 1979, p. 14.

What is Fiction?

Zable, Arnold, 'Fiction or Non Fiction', in *Write On*, Vol. 10, No. 11, 1999, pp. 8–9.

Tolstoy, as quoted by Elisabeth Wynhausen, 'Ordinary People, Unusual Fiction', *The National Times*, 15 April 1983, p. 29.

Lentricchia, Frank, 'My Secret Life with Literature', in *The Australian*, 13 November 1996, p. 50.

Ideas for Stories and Novels

Naslund, Sena, in Jane Sullivan, 'A Whale of a Time', *The Age* (Saturday Extra), 17 June 2000, p. 9.

Miller, Alex, in Louise Bellamy, 'Faith of a Writer', *The Age* (Saturday Extra), 17 June 2000, p. 7.

Malouf, David, in Helen Daniel, 'An Interview with David Malouf', *Australian Book Review*, September 1996, p. 11.

Swift, Graham, in Caroline Baum, 'Possessed by Loves Past and Present', *Weekend Australian*, 5 September 1992, p. 4.

Ciardi, John, in Donald M. Murray, op. cit., p. 234.

Davison, Liam, 'A Writer's Occupation', *Write On*, Vol. 10, No. 11, 1999, p. 13.

Leavitt, David, 'Gravity', in Joyce Carol Oates (ed.), *The Oxford Book of American Short Stories*, Oxford University Press, New York, 1992, p. 741.

Capote, Truman, 'My Side of the Matter', in James Moffett and Kenneth R. McElheny (eds), *Points of View*, Mentor/Penguin Books, New York, 1995, p. 189.

O'Connor, Flannery, cited in Raymond Carver, op. cit., p. 18.

Swift, Graham, cited in Caroline Baum, op. cit., p. 4.

Hall, Rodney, *Quadrant*, Vol. 27, No. 8, 1983, pp. 79–80.

Tolstoy, *Anna Karenina*, Penguin Books, Harmondsworth, 1975, p. 13.

Chekhov, Anton, in Eugene Current-Garcia and Walton R. Patrick (eds), *What is the Short Story?* (rev. edn), Scott Foresman, Chicago, 1974, p. 98.

Character

Galsworthy, John, cited in Douglas A. Hughes, 'Character and Theme', in Douglas A. Hughes, *Studies in Short Fiction*, Holt Rinehart Winston, New York, 1974, p. 529.

Tyler, Anne, from 'A Conversation with Anne Tyler' (unpaginated addendum), in Anne Tyler, *A Patchwork Planet*, Fawcett, New York, 1999.

Winton, Tim, *The Riders*, Pan Macmillan, Sydney, 1995, p. 16.

Austen, Jane, *Emma*, Oxford University Press, Oxford, 1995, p. 3.

Estleman, Loren, *Silent Thunder*, Pan Macmillan, London, 1990, p. 34.

Barnes, Julian, in Rod Usher, 'Barnes by Any Other Name', *The Age* (Saturday Extra), 9 April 1988, p. 10.

Disher, Garry, *The Stencil Man*, HarperCollins, Sydney, 1988, 1999, pp. 116–117.

Disher, Garry, 'Chain', in *The Difference to Me*, HarperCollins, Sydney, 1988, p. 118.

Porter, Katherine Anne, in Eugene Current-Garcia and Walton R. Patrick, op. cit., p. 98.

Dialogue

Disher, Garry, *The Stencil Man*, op. cit., p. 57.

Point of View

Doctorow, E. L., in Phillip McCarthy, 'The New Yorker', *The Age* (Saturday Extra), 9 July 1994, p. 7.

Disher, Garry, *The Divine Wind*, Hodder Headline, Sydney, 1998, London, 1999, pp. 52–54.

Disher, Garry, 'Airship', in *Flamingo Gate: A Novella and Stories*, HarperCollins, Sydney, 1991, pp. 24–25.

Disher, Garry, *The Apostle Bird*, Hodder Headline, Sydney, 1997, pp. 68–69.

Ford, Richard, 'Reading', in David Halpern (ed.), *Antaeus: Literature as Pleasure*, Collins Harvill, London, 1990, p. 45.

Plot

Forster, E. M., from *Aspects of the Novel*, as cited in Douglas A. Hughes, op. cit., p. 533.

Greene, Graham, in Donald M. Murray, op. cit., p. 237.

Ondaatje, Michael, in Mick Brown, op. cit., p. 50.

Hawkes, John, quoted by Scott Turow, 'The Law of Being a Bestseller', *Sunday Age*, 9 January 2000, p. 12.

Planning

Ellroy, James, *Mean Streets*, No. 3, May 1991, p. 25.

McCullough, Colleen, in Diane Armstrong, 'Profile: Colleen McCullough', *Australian Author*, Vol. 27, No. 4, 1996, p. 20.

Irving, John, *Australian Author*, Vol. 22, No. 2, 1991, pp. 15–19.

Foster, David, 'Red Band Adventures', *Australian Author*, Vol. 31, No. 2, 1999, p. 8.

Structure

Malouf, David, in Helen Daniel, op. cit., p. 11.

Barthelme, Donald, cited in William Stone, Nancy Packer and Robert Hoopes (eds), *The Short Story: An Introduction*, McGraw Hill, New York, 1976, p. 568.

Lessing, Doris, 'To Room Nineteen', from *Stories*, Knopf, New York, 1978, p. 396.

Jolley, Elizabeth, 'Pear Tree Dance', from *Woman in a Lampshade*, Penguin Books, Ringwood, 1983, p. 1.

Hulme, Keri, 'Te Kaihau/The Windeater', in Fergus Barrowman, *The Picador Book of Contemporary New Zealand Fiction*, Picador, London, 1996, p. 231.

Disher, Garry, *The Divine Wind*, op. cit., p. 1.

Ahlberg, Allan, in Lyn Gardner, 'Stories from the Cigar Box', *The Guardian*, 24 June 2000, p. 11.

Malouf, David, in Helen Daniel, op. cit., p. 11.

Malouf, David, 'Bad Blood', from *Antipodes*, The Hogarth Press, London, 1985, p. 95.

Setting

Brande, Dorothea, *Becoming a Writer*, Macmillan, London, 1996, p. 106.

Crane, Stephen, 'The Open Boat', in Stone, Parker and Hoopes, op. cit., p. 252.

Davison, Liam, op. cit., p. 13.

Writing a Short Story

Woolf, Virginia, as cited in Stone, Packer and Hoopes, op. cit., p. 216.

Poe, Edgar Allan, ibid., p. 5.

Helprin, Mark (ed.), *The Best American Short Stories 1988*, Houghton Mifflin, New York, 1988, p. xxiv.

Disher, Garry, 'Restoration', from *The Difference to Me*, op. cit., pp. 87–93.

Munro, Alice, cited by Lori Miller, in 'I Know Where the Rope is Attached', *The New York Times Book Review*, 4 September 1986, p. 7.

Paley, Grace, as quoted in Ann Hulbert, 'New Wives Tales', *New York Review of Books*, 11 August 1994, p. 24.

Carver, Raymond, op. cit., p. 9.

Writing a Novel

McEwan, Ian, *The New Review*, Vol. 5, No. 2, 1978, p. 21.

The Words on the Page

Hemingway, Ernest, in Donald M. Murray, op. cit., p. 238.

Murnane, Gerald, Melbourne Writers' Festival, August 1988.

Naipaul, V. S., in Gordon Burns, 'The Gospel According to Naipaul', *Weekend Australian*, 9–10 July 1994, p. 4.

Tan, Amy, 'Gloom, Doom and the Second Book', *Weekend Australian*, 20–21 July 1991, p. 3.

Flaubert, Gustave, in Donald M. Murray, op. cit., p. 236.

'Rules for Newspaper Writers', ibid., p. 101.

Bail, Murray, *Holden's Performance*, Viking, Ringwood, 1987, pp. 12–13.

Mansfield, Katherine, in Donald M. Murray, op. cit., p. 240.

Hemingway, Ernest and Didion, Joan, *The New Yorker*, 4 August 1998, p. 74.

Munro, Alice, 'Miles City, Montana', from *The Progress of Love*, Chatto and Windus, London, 1987, p. 84.

Nabokov, Vladimir, as quoted by Patricia Hampl, 'The Lax Habits of the Imagination', *The New York Times Book Review*, 5 March 1989, p. 38.

Borges, Jorge Luis, as quoted by John Dale, *The Australian's Review of Books*, Vol. 1, No. 3, 1996, p. 26.

Troubleshooting

Paretsky, Sara, in Mary Ann Metcalf, 'Making Sense of the Senseless', *Sisters in Crime Newsletter*, No. 7, Summer, 1994, p. 4.

Chekhov, Anton, in Eugene Current-Garcia and Walton R. Patrick, op. cit., p. 22.

Disher, Garry, 'Judge's Report' (unpub.), 1999.

Ford, Richard, in Jason Steger, 'The Word Servant', *The Age* (Saturday Extra), 18 March 2000, p. 3.